# MASTERING
## THE ART OF
# MASTERY

# MASTERING
## THE ART OF
# MASTERY

### Raven Kaldera

**Alfred Press**
Hubbardston, Massachusetts

**Alfred Press**
12 Simond Hill Road
Hubbardston, MA 01452

**Mastering the Art of Mastery**
© 2020 Raven Kaldera
ISBN 978-0-9905441-7-3

Printed in cooperation with
Lulu Enterprises, Inc.
Morrisville, NC 27560

*Dedicated to Lady Lynette
for inspiring me*

# Contents

# Introduction: The Art of Mastery

Yes, it really is an art. It's also a crapshoot, a roller coaster ride, a skydiving adventure ... and a quiet snuggle on the couch. It's exhilarating, frustrating, scary, confidence-building, and comforting. It's all those things plus what you make of it. What we hope it won't be, for you, is disastrous. This book is our hope that you will raise your chances of success, if only a little.

When I started out, I had a mixed bag of experience. I'd worked for myself—and *by* myself—since I was in my twenties; I'd never been a boss in a formal work situation. I held a position of authority in my church, but it was more the sort of position that one gains because no one else wants it, and my ability to get church volunteers to cooperate on anything that required effort or caused inconvenience was low. I hadn't been raised with wealth and privilege—quite the opposite, really—and my only experience of personal service was the usual brief interaction with waitstaff and cashiers. On the other hand, I'd been a parent, and while s-types are adults and not children, I did learn a lot from the experience that carried over, including that all-important point of being in charge of someone else's entire life. (I have often told my slaveboy that nothing he's ever done has made me tear out my hair as much as dealing with teenagers during the rebellion phase when they hate their parents on principle.) I'd also read a lot about history, and absorbed many ideas about how service was done in past eras. (Some of this would be useful and some of it would be counterproductive.) And, of course, I had a very dominant, pushy personality, and I enjoyed being in charge. I was good at taking on responsibility, and not afraid of it at all.

Taking on a full-time slave, and the process of finding my feet with the power dynamic, reminded me in many ways of when I and my senior partner had bought our small homestead-farm. I'd interned on such a small homestead-farm, and learned skills ranging from gardening to composting to canning to milking goats to slaughtering chickens. I was reasonably sure that I would be able to make it work. Once we got the land and the old farmhouse, however, we realized that the first hundred things that needed to happen were all in the category of carpentry and home improvement. The house needed lots of repairs and renovations, the barn hadn't been home to anything but junk in a long time, the fences had crumbled, and the chicken house had fallen to pieces.

For a full year, all we did was build and rebuild things, and I came face to face with a whole raft of skills that it hadn't occurred to me that I would need. I scrambled to learn, drove a lot of crooked nails, ruined a fair amount of screws, and put up a lot of drywall with hastily-tacked-up trim over poorly-spackled seams. Fortunately, my senior partner was in the same boat and trying just as hard, and we were able to be patient with each other. However, it was an equal partnership between us. Had one of us been dependent on the other, things might have been much more difficult.

Before I'd acquired a human being who was willing to let me run his life, I'd been a BDSM dominant. What that had meant, for me, was that I took on responsibility for submissive sex partners during scenes. As soon as the scene was over, so was my authority. Sometimes the dominance and submission would bleed into more general areas of life. Sometimes that went well, but more often than not it ended up going wrong, because I didn't understand how the negotiation for non-scene power and authority was completely different from that of scene power and authority. I was also ignorant of how it should be accomplished. The other dominants in the local BDSM scene had what I would call "play slaves"—submissives who would enact various levels of obedience during play parties or specific "dates", but they would have been horrified by the idea that you could run someone's life down to their career or medical care or how they ought to vote.

Later—several years after my slaveboy and I had fumbled our way to a reasonably healthy and functional power dynamic—I met a number of masters who were doing what we were trying to do, and beginning to talk about it. Our first visit to the newly formed local chapter of MAsT (Masters And slaves Together, a power exchange support group) was eye-opening. We were not the newest people in the room by any stretch of the imagination by then, but it was fascinating to see other people who were doing what we were doing in ways that were slightly to exceptionally different. Later, we would go to the newly emerging power exchange national conferences and see an even wider array of couples (and triples, and families). It broadened our horizons and gave us language to more eloquently describe our process. It also gave us tips and tricks for the hard bits, some of which we'd been struggling with for years and still hadn't been able to overcome.

If, when I'd started out, I'd had other M-types around to give me rational advice on what common obstacles I'd be likely to run into—and reassure me that the ones we were already tripping on were, indeed, common—it would have saved me a huge amount of time and effort. I know that not everyone has access to this kind of human contact, especially when you're just starting out. This book is my gift to you, the one I wished I'd had. It's my attempt to make your lives and your processes just a little bit easier.

Some of the essays within are written by me; others are written by a number of wonderful and competent masters and dominant partners from all walks of life. The have one thing in common—they all have at least one other human being who trusts them to tell them what to do, in part or in whole. They've been down the road of M-type rookie mistakes, and they are here to give you the map. While we can't cover every situation in which you might find yourself stuck, we can mark out a lot of the swamps and thornbushes, the cracked deserts and tangled forests and flooding rivers. If you don't yet have a submissive or slave as a partner, and you are wise enough to know that any big job is worth preparing for, you'll find plenty of good potential curriculum in here. Take it and begin your journey of power and responsibility ... because those two qualities always need to balance each other out.

Good luck,

Raven Kaldera
July 2020

# Qualities of a Good Master

*Joshua Tenpenny*[*]

I wrote this list for someone who wished to be a master and wanted to know what qualities to cultivate, but it serves equally well as qualities for a submissive to look for when seeking a master. To simply be a master, you only need a strong will and some skills in understanding people—how they work and what motivates them—in order to get them to do what you want. Charisma, arrogance, formal protocol, and general "domliness" may convince the casual observer that you are a good master, but I think it takes a little more than that. If someone is to freely offer their entire life over to another person, shouldn't they expect a bit more of them than charm and a full toybag? Being a good master is more than being a good person; it is being a good person when in complete control of another.

Obviously, different people hold different standards, but here are some qualities I personally would expect of a good master (or mistress). They are in no particular order, and I've randomly alternated the genders throughout.

❖ He has impeccable honor. He has a clearly defined moral code and he actually lives by it. While he needn't be completely perfect, he needs to be significantly better than most people in this in order to be trusted with complete control over another person. He is well aware of any areas where he has difficulty holding consistently to his moral code, and he is always working to improve. He recognizes quickly when he has acted dishonorably, and seeks to make amends in whatever way he can.

❖ She can clearly state her core values and priorities, and her words and actions reflect them. When her priorities are unflattering, she is honest with herself about them, even if she chooses to keep them private.

❖ His philosophical and/or spiritual beliefs, especially with regard to honor, responsibility, leadership, and service, are sincerely held and not merely self-serving. He has some concept of something

---

[*] Reprinted from *Real Service*, Alfred Press 2011.

greater than his personal will or ego, if only the common good of society.

❖ She acts honorably when she has "real world" power over someone, such as her children, pets, or employees. She treats service personnel with courtesy, and is comfortable receiving personal service. She is not derisive towards or made uncomfortable by people of a lower social station.

❖ He acts honorably when someone has "real world" power over him. Even if he dislikes acting under anyone else's direction, it does not make him irrational or petty. He acts politely and reasonably to his boss, police officers, judges, and the like. He is not derisive towards or made uncomfortable by people of a higher social station.

❖ She knows her limitations and failings, and she can respond maturely to someone pointing them out even when they do so rudely. She genuinely appreciates constructive criticism from an appropriate source, even when it is difficult for her to hear.

❖ He knows what he wants and makes no apologies for it. He knows the difference between what he wants and what he can have, and he handles such disappointments with maturity. He does not feel excessive guilt or discomfort about desiring control over another person, and he feels he can act on these feelings without violating his ethical or spiritual beliefs.

❖ She knows clearly the difference between fantasy and reality, and can function in reality. She knows the difference between truth and fiction, and she is honest unless she has good reason not to be. She knows the difference between telling lies, being honestly mistaken, and being willfully ignorant, both in reference to her own statements and those of others. She operates under a fairly internally consistent logic that is in harmony with her perception of reality. She is not actively mentally ill in any significant way.

❖ He has no addictions, obsessions, or compulsions that seriously interfere with his ability to make decisions.

❖ She takes responsibility for her words and actions. In crisis, she doesn't look first for someone or something to blame. She understands and accepts the consequences of her actions, both long and short term.

❖ He understands that the best plans fail occasionally, even when every possible effort has been made, and that no one is perfect. He can do honest risk assessment and make back-up plans, and cope with failures maturely and constructively.

❖ She has her life in good order, for the most part, and does not live crisis to crisis. She does not seem to invite turmoil into her life without good reason.

❖ He is reliable. If he says he will do something, you can trust that he will make every effort to do it. If he knows there is a significantly higher than normal chance of failure in a plan, he strives to make this clear beforehand to the parties concerned.

❖ Her judgment is sound. She makes better choices than most in tough situations, and is not paralyzed by difficult or unpleasant choices. She has good reasons for her decisions, regardless of whether she explains them to others.

❖ He understands his emotions and copes with them reasonably well. He has someone in his life with whom he can express his emotions, even if only a therapist or clergyperson.

❖ She controls her temper flawlessly. She does not act on sadistic urges (emotional or physical) in inappropriate ways, even under stress. She does not respond violently without serious physical provocation.

Some people may put more emphasis on different points of character, or have more or less flexibility in certain areas, but I feel the really important thing is to have some idea of what you personally think makes for a good master, beyond the basic ability to inspire someone to do as you say. One can be extremely good at extracting obedience and be a fairly reprehensible person. There are very few real psychos out there, but there are many irresponsible and self-centered individuals who can cause a great deal of damage to a person who is so vulnerable to them. If slaves are to find honor in their service, they must do it by serving honorable masters.

# Preparing Yourself For Mastery

*Raven Kaldera*

I see a lot of would-be masters asking about what they can do, while they are still waiting or searching for the right slave to come into their lives, to prepare themselves for mastery. Sometimes they are still young—while some people might laugh at an 18-year-old who wants to be a master, I remember what I was like at that age. I wasn't ready for it emotionally, and I had been fed a lot of opinions about how such a thing was wrong, but if I'd had a sympathetic and useful role model, I'd certainly have put it on my list of life goals.

The problem is that even if you know about M/s (or O/p, or even lifestyle D/s) and have models of what it's like on a realistic level, that doesn't mean that you will be able to walk out and find yourself a slave. Even if you find one, you may not be able to make the relationship work out if you don't have any preparation for it. When you have authority exchange, you're playing with fire. The higher the level of authority exchange, the hotter the flames, and the more potential for both parties getting burned. Before you are able to juggle flaming torches, it's good to learn to juggle non-flaming torches.

Many M/s people say that the skills necessary for M/s or O/p relationships are the same skills needed for egalitarian relationships. I find that most of the people saying this are s-types, and I strongly disagree. Just because you can talk to a partner doesn't mean that you're going to be a good leader—and one of the good things about egalitarian relationships is that both parties have equal ability to step in and get in the other person's face if they're making major mistakes. In an inegalitarian relationship, by definition one person is far more vulnerable to the other person's mistakes, and has far less recourse. The person in charge has got to be better at it than the average egalitarian partner, because more is resting on their shoulders, and the ability to seriously hurt someone is higher.

So I've made a list of ways that a would-be master can prepare themselves. This isn't a quick, short course of action. It may take a lifetime.

❖ Get leadership training. You can take classes on that, or get officer's training if you join the military. However, one of the best ways to get practice is to join a struggling non-profit organization, volunteer for a while until you're a fixture (which, given the turnover with most volunteer non-profits, won't be long), and then volunteer to run and organize something where you're in charge of a number of people. It's good to learn how to lead people who aren't obligated to do what you say *before* you lead someone who is. (If you're already in a leadership position with your job, see if your workplace will send you to formal leadership training.) The idea is to learn how to inspire people to get things done, rather than just ordering them in a harsh voice and hoping that works. Learning how to inspire followers is an invaluable skill for being a master. Really.

❖ Babysit. No, really, for real. (Assuming that you are not the primary caretaker of your own children, in which case you've already got this one.) Obviously, adult s-types are not children, but taking care of someone else's kids is good practice for two reasons. First, it gives you a chance to experience the state of having a vulnerable dependent for a long period of time, where everything you do must be cross-checked with "How is this going to affect them?" Second, it gives you the chance to gently get stubborn souls that you're not allowed to beat (one assumes) into line.

❖ Do research. Read different nonfiction books on power exchange. Talk to people who are in power dynamics and ask them questions. Join support groups if there are any in your area. Get different perspectives, so that you can figure out what you want and don't want. Make lists of what services, rituals, protocols, and behaviors sound good to you, and why they seem attractive. (There is a booklist at the end of this book in case you are completely new to this and not sure where to look for resources.)

❖ Practice being patient and non-reactive when things go wrong. Figure out something you can do in under five seconds that gives you a quick calm-down-and-get-clear. I use breathing exercises, or I sing a specific little song to myself. Then I ask myself: *What is actually going on here, from an objective perspective?* Or I might ask myself, *What's scary here? What am I afraid of happening next?* I'm doing this instead of freaking out or yelling. If you can slowly build in this sort of reaction when things go wrong, it can be a huge help for future relationship conflict when it's your job to be calm and make good decisions in the face of your own strong emotions.

❖ Practice listening to people, especially people who are saying things you're not invested in. You can practice with friends— ask them to talk about something that's important to them but that you're not interested in. Make yourself pay attention to what they're saying, and don't interrupt them unless it is necessary to ask for more information. Reiterate what they said back to them, to make sure you understood it. Practicing this skill can make an s-type feel like you hear them and actually care about their problem, as opposed to blowing them off.

❖ For that matter, any conflict resolution skills you can learn will help. There are classes and trainings in such things; don't underestimate how useful those are. Don't think that just because you have authority over someone means that there will never be any conflict. You may be able to make rules about how that conflict manifests, but you'll still have relationship disagreements, and sometimes those will be passionate and furious.

❖ Learn to set boundaries that are firm but compassionate, both for yourself (if you tend toward giving too much) and for the other person (if you tend toward setting boundaries in a state of anger or resentment). Learn to set them in a reasonable way *before* you become overwhelmed and react.

❖ Most importantly, get your shit in a pile. By that I mean that you should be reasonably stable both in the practical world and the emotional world. You don't have to be rich or perfect, but your life should not be constantly in crisis. If this requires therapy or peer support, do it. If you have major psychological baggage in your life that seriously affects your decision-making and personal interactions, work on that. Rather than coming to the table of power exchange pretending to have your life together, use this time to actually work on it and get it together for real. The more self-aware and solvent you are, the better a Master you will make.

# E-G-O Is Not How You Spell Master

*Mistress Sky*

The most important lesson that a would-be master can learn is that an egocentric self-identity is a poor foundation for the responsibilities of being a dominant in an unequal relationship. The reader can consult many psychology books on the "ego" and its influence, but for the sake of this essay let's define the word "ego" as a one-word reference to a skewed and unrealistically elevated perspective on oneself. "Ego-centered" or "egocentric" or "self-absorbed" are helpful phrases that describe a dominant in an unequal relationship who does not prioritize the good health of the whole. Of course, someone can be controlling and/or self-centered and still be focused on the good of the relationship. Being self-absorbed and acting from ego is, however, a blindness that assures a less than wonderful relationship for all parties involved. Both partners will get more and thrive better if they stay focused on maintaining the good health of their unequal relationship. What you will read here offers a structural check-up for the reader in the interest of improving unequal relationships. For purposes of this article, we will assume that every M (dominant, master, mistress, daddy, mommy or leading partner) wants to be the best M that he or she can be. We will also assume that every M cares for their submissive or slave and wants the best possible conditions for that partner.

### It Wasn't Your Idea to Follow Ego

Where did the ego-led identity come from? Society, of course. We won't spend a lot of time on the Where or the How, but it is easy to see far too many examples of misguided ideas about leadership in the world. Here are a few that you might recognize:

❖ As a core element of what it means to lead, a leader dictates to others how they are to behave. The follower has no choice but to do as they are told.

❖ To be in the lead position in a relationship means that you are the one who matters most, so of course your needs are given primacy over all others at all times. Sacrifices on the submissive's or slave's part are to be expected.

❖ The leader's control is absolute, so nothing he or she does is considered a mistake.

❖ And, of course, the leader knows everything. The leader has all the right answers all the time.

❖ The leader listens to the subordinate to some extent but has no intention of learning from a subordinate, who is lower in status than them.

Every day, these wretched ideas are pushed on our unequal relationships from the larger society. No dominant partner is immune from being a carrier of bad ideas or harmful enculturation, but not one of these miserable assumptions is supportive or healthy in an unequal relationship. We should laugh at them—and at ourselves—and move on.

## Mastery of the Self

One myth about mastery contains a kernel of truth that I like to keep in mind. It's that the concept "mastery" refers to mastery of the self/Self. It has nothing to do with finding ways to make someone do your bidding. If you wish to be someone's dominant partner, then self-control, self-awareness, and self-development are the "mastery" to which to commit yourself, and this will be a lifelong process and commitment. Defined as such, a Master is an honorable being that others will want to follow.

If a male M holds that the unequal relationship exists to celebrate his manhood, to elevate his maleness, and punctuate his male superiority, then he has chosen a weak foundation for his own life and for that unequal relationship. If any of those sound pretty good to you, then consider that these thoughts do not serve your relationship if it is to be healthy. Consider, too, that it's okay to have a bit of ego rubbing (otherwise known as pride) and a sense of self-importance. But these feel-good treats should be coincidental by-products of solid work that the dominant has done to create and maintain a wonderful, healthy, sustainable unequal status with a terrific partner. In other words: If you, the dominant, believe that the primary purpose of the unequal relationship is to help you to feel bigger, then you have cheated the relationship, your partner, and yourself.

These kinds of unequal relationships are noted for degrading or beating down the submissive partner, physically or emotionally. Supposedly, by putting down the slave, the M feels uplifted. The dominant partner may also evaluate the relationship by how turned on they felt by some action the slave was ordered to do. However, as responsible leaders in an intimate relationship, we want to make a more credible assessment of how things are going. We need to turn to better evidence, such as:

❖ Ask your partner. Listen to your partner.
❖ Take an honest look at the mechanics of the relationship. Ask your partner to be examining with you: good communication, agreements adhered to, negotiating repeatedly as needed, setting relationship goals and meeting them, rituals and protocols only as needed to support the relationship.

The healthy, truly consensual unequal partnership is meant to sustain and uplift you both, not one person—you—over another.

> *Master Carissa and her slave, Kelin, routinely hold household discussions on Sunday evenings, and only after the weekly ritual of worshipping all things chocolate.*

Note that "unequal" can be a positive, even loving, term that refers to a truly consensual, strongly desired and mutually achieved slant in power and control in a personal relationship. It's a jointly held and maintained relationship state with an intention of benefiting each and every partner.

### You Can Choose to Honor the Relationship

If the M's cultural background includes a heavy dose of individualism (typical of American culture, and of most male culture, which has a significant influence on every gender) then it is going to take a great deal of self-awareness to be able to make the best choices for the good of the unequal relationship. Think of individualism as ego's twin. Without serious introspection and commitment, the M is likely to attempt to continue what he or she knows best—singularity—in spite of the communal or partnership life setting of an unequal relationship. That one element can cause immediate discord in communication with one's partner. Each of you may be using similar language and still be at odds because you are divided in your overall goal. The dominant just wants what is already familiar and comfortable and what is not a challenge to his/her authority. That's all. The submissive wants to please the M, of course, but in ways that are inclusive of the submissive's needs. Even the most emotionally masochistic s-type wants a feeling of satisfaction through service to their dominant. But what if the dominant isn't in union with the s-type about service to the whole, for the good of the relationship?

*Ms. Caretha misinterpreted her girl slave's attempts to offer information or the slave's differing opinion as necessarily challenges to her authority.*

The right question to ask is what each of you wants from the unequal relationship. Discussions should focus there. Time to negotiate (again).

With or without individualism at issue, the M may have the mistaken idea that we dominants are perfect, and we do not make mistakes. "It's weak and compromising to my dominance to admit to having an issue or deficit." This is really about status and appearance. *How do others regard me? Am I seen as the big, mighty, all-knowing dominant that I think that I am?* The ego-centered M is insecure and persistently worried about how they are being seen by their submissive and by other dominants. The opposite character is a secure and peaceful M who can locate their security within the relationship itself. The unequal relationship's good health is your foundation.

You and your ego matter the most? Really? Well, we do imagine ourselves as actors in our own Unequal Relationship play, for sure. However, given that we are dealing with real human lives—yours and your partner(s)—the way that you inject your energy and personality must serve the good of the relationship or doing harm becomes a possibility. Think about your own very fine talents, amazing attributes and skills, and your good intentions applied to a magnificent relationship that you and your partner(s) can be proud of. You will be justifiably proud given that you've actually worked to build something great. Ego is only along for the ride.

Maybe in fiction, leadership equals dictatorship. Do you feel that your job is to make others do what you want? Are your methods coercion, manipulation, deceit, and force? These are personal weaknesses. You and your partner(s) are a team, a unit, and possibly a nesting group and, of course, you expect to lead your group to heavenly success. The best leaders do not reduce their own leadership to crude, base activities like yelling or ruling with fear or expecting the other person to just magically know what you want and how you want it. Leadership has to be about so much more. Leadership has to be created out of the truth of who you are inside. If it's not the Real You, then the relationship already has a built in, fundamental weakness. It's okay to let go of old misconceptions about what it means to lead. You can replace those misguided ideas with the real deal of your own strengths. Following through on your responsibilities in an unequal relationship is an opportunity to examine what you have and to claim all of your best traits as strengths.

### We All Have More to Learn

Yet another consequence of egocentrism in our unequal relationships is failing to see the value of the s-type as a teacher. Ego can get in the way of clear vision and the M may have trouble allowing himself to learn from his s-type. Each partner has had their unique set of life experiences and lessons learned, and they have plenty of perspective to offer their dominant. The M needs put all the resources these experiences represent to work for the good of the relationship. To do otherwise is to ignore valuable assets that are at hand and could have been used for effective support. Accepting assistance from your submissive or even being shown how to do something by your slave takes away zero Brownie Points on your Dominant Badge of Honor.

A dominant might assume that there is nothing to learn: "I already know everything." "Everybody tells me that I am a natural at this." Well, good. Be glad that you feel confident. Go ahead and feel good about you being You. Now, advance forward with excellent information about how best to create and then maintain a healthy, sustainable relationship. Accepting new information is to your credit. "A leader learns" should be your new mantra. To do otherwise would be like insisting on maintaining a still and stagnant pond. Bodies of water need refreshing if they are to be healthy, and so do relationships. Relationships, if they are to be healthy, must have movement within them that originates from outside the partners. Where are you getting your fresh inputs to contribute to your healthy unequal relationship?

So let's talk about credible knowledge sources for you. First, look around for your kink community's hub. It might be a local nightclub or dungeon. It might be less obvious because local people meet at munches (public Meet-and-Greets that are not sexual or kinky), which are usually held in restaurants. Go. Meet. Make new friends. Allow yourself to become part of the community. Try to be a useful servant of the community by volunteering. If your community offers classes, then follow what interests you. If your community offers a Meet-Up for mentors and mentees, then please, attend. Learn. Pay attention. Enjoy. Practice being part of a larger whole without falling back on presenting as the Big Guy or Gal that Everyone Must Applaud.

Second, you can read the legitimate literature that is now available on unequal relationships. You'll find a few authors listed at the end of this book. The names listed are authors who have published an actual relationship model as opposed to books that state a handful of relationship ideas. No relationship model is perfect for every individual nor should it be expected to be. Find the model that resonates with who you are. Do not treat any book as a recipe for how to do your life; instead, study several models, decide which one sounds like you, discuss it with your (potential) partners, and then make it your own by only using the model as a guiding influence. Make your own decisions for the good of your relationship, and don't be afraid of trial and error. Once you discover what kind of dominance in which relationship model that you are drawn to, that might help you tremendously to find the right s-type for you. It will probably help you to be more articulate about your vision for an unequal relationship <u>and</u> better able to listen deeply to your partner's or potential partner's needs.

## Ego Effects on Connection to Others and the World

Connection to another human being is a magnificent phenomenon and a blessing, and in these relationships, it is the dominant partner's job to steward it. Every dominant in an unequal relationship should believe this, but is every dominant honoring it as such?

Consider your connection to your unequal relationship and, therefore, to your partner. The dominant is <u>in</u> the relationship, not outside of it. How you affect or influence the health of the relationship is very direct and very immediate. See yourself and partner as active participants located inside the container of whatever agreements you hold together. Those agreements are malleable—you negotiated them at the beginning—but going forward you may end up negotiating again and again, initiated by either of you.

It's much too easy for the dominant to see himself/herself as separate and apart from their s-type and that attitude is always problematic. If the dominant imagines his/her position as high and lofty then their position in the relationship is emotionally distant. If that is what you insist upon, then your decision-making is also going to be made from a distance. More distance in attitude and mental stance equals less effective decision-making due to poor information about what is needed. Come down from the mountain sometimes to better gauge what's really going on.

Even the word "partner" implies that you and the s-type are doing the relationship together. Stay close and regard your partner with high regard in order to receive the best information about what the relationship needs are that you must consider. Only then can you take good measure of the quality of the relationship. From a position of closeness, you can lead yourself and partner through whatever changes or modifications or new agreements that best suit your relationship at any given time. Closeness equals strength.

Some dominants, male or female, do not see their actions as being connected to anything or anyone else; they have no thoughts of contributing to others except as a display of ego. Such a personality is a Taker with a likely belief in "survival of the fittest" and "the strongest survive." Whatever successes these M's have in the world can only be explained, in their minds, by their prowess. They believe that nothing is owed to society, or to the natural world, and that nothing is owed within the relationship. The danger here is likely a lack of accountability. The question need to be asked: to whom is their accountability for the actions of the dominant in an unequal relationship?

The M may have trouble letting down internal walls and letting the s-type come closer. Perhaps, the dominant, male or female, is fearful of conceding some power or some control. When exactly does holding power or control have to be absolute? This is likely a paradox of wanting very much to be seen as you really are and at the same time being afraid to be seen for fear of being judged to be unworthy or lacking or just not good enough. The bigger problem here is that the dominant may have trouble letting the sub or slave use their talents to give service.

> A female dominant has recently acquired a male slave and moved him into her house. He and her children get along very well and everyone seems to be settling in as a happy family unit. Every day, he offers her service in forms that are acceptable to her but sometimes she stops him without explanation. She had been running her life and raising her children with little help from anyone for several years, and she reports that it is difficult to release even a little bit of control. She admits that even a small shift in control could mean being able to better relax in her own home, and letting her slave take really good care of her.

Dominants may find themselves stumbling forward because of inadequate communication with their slave. It is necessary, and it will always be necessary, to check on the consequences of the resulting situation after some great command of yours has been given. Otherwise, how can you have accurate information about how the relationship is progressing at that moment? For better communication between partners, use the simple device called "trial and error" plus correction. What if your lack of explanations prevented the job from getting done and, in fact, left the s-type flailing about and lost? Ego and pridefulness are poor elements in a dominant's reactions to their s-type's need for clarification. A wiser action might look like taking a breath and recalibrating how best to communicate what's needed. Did your explanation and request include making sure your submissive knows what the ultimate goal is? Sometimes, giving context for why you want the food on the table by 7 p.m. tonight helps both you and the s-type to make things go smoothly. Paying attention to how we communicate so that we can repeat what works best is part of our job as dominants/leading partners/heads of household. Making adjustments to how you make requests or issue directives is not an affront to your sovereignty.

Regarding communication, some dominants might ask, "Why aren't my directives to my sub enough? Why must I explain? My definition of dominance does not include training the s-type. Why should I be inconvenienced in any way?" That's the voice of ego. A more reasonable voice would be reminding you that all relationships require work. You must do your share, even if you are claiming to be the one in charge. Leading must include such things as paying attention, being fully present for your partner instead of only presenting a scattered mind, noticing what works for the two of you, and accepting responsibility for how the relationship is going.

### The Ego-Charged Perspective Is A Skewed Vision

History and society has certainly given us our fill of hierarchy in the most negative sense (nonconsensual slavery, male dominance over resources and positions of real power, disregard for the disabled, the devaluing of children and of those who take care of children) and that negativity is going to be found even in our alternative relationship models. The dominant may not even realize that his innermost mind actually regards the submissive as "less than." The M assumes that everyone wants to be the dominant. That's an ego-voice speaking. There's more—the idea that the slave would be an M if only they had it in them to be so. Society has social contempt for submissiveness, so this M assumes it must be bad, or at least not preferred. "It sucks to be you; your saving grace in life is that you are lucky enough to have me as your dominant. That makes you less worthless."

Sometimes, this kind of ego-twisted view of s-types is evidenced in repeated loyalty tests for the sub or slave: "If you were truly loyal to me, as you should be, you would do X." This often turns out to be a coercive trick, a manipulation, especially if X is something demeaning and not healthy for the sub or slave, but the M does not care about that so long as their ego gets a positive hit. Here is one example:

> *A female slave lives in the home of her male master. She has specific chores to take care of his/their home. He greatly enjoys having sex parties in their home. She knows that she will be asked to do sex acts during these parties which are definitely not to her liking, but she will do them as a demonstration of her devotion to her master. Her master knows that she is heterosexual so his repeated requirement that she lick a female guest's clitoris is very pleasing to him and acceptable as a gift of her devotion. The female slave feels satisfied each time that she has pleased her master and that has to be enough for her.*

You have choices. Be truly present for your unequal partner(s). Challenge yourself to be an engaged, caring listener, and realize how much you can learn from a submissive. Honor the life that they have entrusted you to care for, and be humbled by their trust. Challenge yourself to see the s-type as the magnificent human being that they are. The slave's or submissive's compulsion to serve is the complement to *your* service as their dominant.

### Be the Visionary

*Being visionary* and *coming from a place of ego* are an unfortunate pairing that do not, in real life, work well together. Ego can steer a dominant toward haughtiness and emotional distance. Any vision of how valuable the unequal relationship is can be obscured by the size of the dominant's ego. Having vision for the sake of the relationship is not a problem, but manufacturing that vision separate and apart from one's partner's perspectives is. Having ideas about the direction of the relationship is to be applauded, but not in isolation from the partner. Envisioning together can only be a boon to the relationship becoming everything that you both need it to be.

Envisioning might look like a light, informal conversation as you walk along a park path and take in the evening air. Envisioning is intended to be a great pleasure for you and partner(s). How can it be otherwise since you are jointly giving voice to your ideal conditions for the relationship? What do each of you want if you could have anything?

We dominants should set the right tone for liberated conversation by checking our own attitudes. We do not want to suck up most of the oxygen as we converse with our s-types if we want to hear what is really going on with them. It's better to leave space and oxygen for the s-types to be themselves. Ask yourself: Am I keeping the conversation light and free? Am I encouraging my s-type to talk freely? Am I discouraging heavy leaning on my thoughts and my wishes? Am I being supportive whenever she/he reveals their own original thoughts? Am I staying fully present in the conversation so that I can really hear how the submissive feels? Be sure to follow through for the good of the relationship by making effective use of whatever comes from your mutual envisioning.

### Check Yourself Regularly and Often

Find your healthy, happy community that's serious about power exchange and become actively involved. Practice community membership by noticing what needs to be done to benefit everyone, and volunteer as much as you can. You will benefit. You will learn a lot. Journaling might help you to realize the positive gain for you when you give to others.

Mentorship is a great gift that a community gives itself. Keep your eyes open for very experienced people who are respected in your community. Ask about recommendations for possible mentors. Talk to them. Ask questions. Notice how comfortable (or not) you feel with someone. How trustworthy do you feel this person is? How willing is the person to answer a question or two without any formal commitment of mentorship? You will benefit. Be sure to express appreciation whether you go forward into mentorship or not.

Encourage your s-types to be part of the community and to be surrounded by supportive friends. Avoid contributing to isolation for you or for your slave.

Finally, there is no need to fight the ego—you won't win. Don't try to repress it, either. Even developing anxiety about ego is energy wasted in the wrong direction. Instead, check yourself regularly and often. Are your actions contributing to the good health of the relationship? What is your evidence of that? What healthy outside influences also help to sustain your terrific unequal relationship? How often do you check in with your partner about real needs and how those needs can be handled? When was the last time that you had negotiation discussions? What goals have the two of you set for the relationship? Are you keeping an eye on your progress toward those goals? Commit to making better choices motivated by your strong desire to build and maintain a healthy and wonderful sustainable unequal relationship.

---

*Mistress Sky is a lifestyle domme and presenter at our New England conferences. She is a relationship coach and alternative lifestyle counselor, author, and the founder of Elevate Womxn Collaborative, a women's empowerment organization. To find out more, contact: http://gatescounseling.com.*

# Don't Bottom to Porn! (Or Communities, Either.)

*Raven Kaldera*

Where's the first place that most people see examples of Master/slave relationships? Why, fiction, of course! And probably erotic fiction, if not straight-out pornography. These are in most cases our first exposure to the idea that one person could have authority over the life of another and it could be, if not comfortable, then at least exciting and sexually charged. Fiction on the subject of these sorts of interactions generally come in the following varieties:

❖ Hardcore pornography and softcore romance about modern people engaging in (often barely) negotiated hierarchical relationships, usually for the primary purpose of kinky sex with some housecleaning and suchlike on the side. Examples: *Mr. Benson*, *Carrie's Story*, Laura Antoniou's *Marketplace* series.

❖ Hardcore pornography and softcore romance about people in historical, fantasy, or science fiction worlds engaging in the same sort of thing, although often without the consent or negotiation. Example: Ann Rice's *Sleeping Beauty* trilogy.

❖ Non-erotic fictional portrayals of dystopian suffering where heartless, evil masters torture innocent slaves. While the authors of these books may actually be working hard to portray such situations as Very Bad And Not Desirable At All, they may have no idea how strong the power of perversion can be. Some people manage to eroticize it anyway. Example: Alex Haley's *Roots*.

❖ What my slaveboy refers to as "butler porn". Stories of historical servitude (butlers, chambermaids, manservants, etc.) where the role is somewhat romanticized, or at least the horrible everyday grind is downplayed. Examples: Downton Abbey, Gosford Park.

❖ Stories of "traditional" marital relationships—meaning couplings based on heterosexual male-dominant female-submissive marriages loaded with unquestioned old-fashioned sexism. These are usually only "softcore" erotica, such as romantic bodice-rippers or adventure stories, and they have been written the same way for centuries. The s-types are always female, and never dissatisfied with the role that society has forced them into. The M-types are always male, and always able to make the right decisions—unless they are villains, in which case the female s-type's job is to suffer until rescued by another male.

The problem here is that erotic fiction—however well written— is not useful advice for having a fulfilling and sustainable relationship. Honestly, how many people would believe that watching or reading vanilla porn is the way to figure out how to have a healthy egalitarian relationship? (Well, there may be a few of them wandering around the world, but they are probably characterized by their extreme lack of loving, committed partners.) In most of these fictional worlds, the masters are filthy rich; this does not aid a couple who are attempting to create power exchange in a trailer park, and it adds to the idea that you can't do this properly if you aren't wealthy. The slaves never get sick, or have menstrual cramps, or become old and too arthritic to kneel. For that matter, the masters never get sick or have menstrual cramps either, and when they get older their slaves do not push their wheelchair, but throw them over for a younger model. Which the masters do as well to aging or "imperfect" slaves.

These stories do not prepare us in any way for the reality of life, and how to handle struggle with external circumstances while keeping a power dynamic skillfully balanced. The slaves are sometimes given an arena in which to struggle and find their strength, but it is almost always an arena created deliberately by their masters for purposes of amusement. (In my experience, real life gives enough actual challenges that it doesn't make sense to deliberately make situations harder.) The masters, however, are never seen struggling (unless they are villain-characters who've just been thrown down by the hero) with real-world challenges such as financial problems or disability, or with their own difficult urges and internal baggage. These stories come with an insidious message: In order to be a master of slaves, or even a leader of followers, you have to be flawlessly competent, or at least pretend to be so in front of your cringing subordinates.

You also have to be somewhat sociopathic. It turns my stomach to note the uncaring and rabidly selfish personalities of masters in much of the BDSM pornography genre. (Male dominants are often wholly psychopathic in their disdain for all human life; female dominants tend toward erratic and emotionally unstable in their violence.) Apparently sociopaths and people with various other personality disorders are erotically attractive when it comes to these stories, and the idea of a master who is kind, thoughtful, compassionate, and aware of social inequities is not sexually or romantically thrilling at all. Even less so is the idea of a master who struggles with anything in their life. In fact, these genres of literature tend to subtly encourage the idea that in order to be a good leader, one *has* to be pretty sociopathic, and the aforementioned qualities would make someone "weak" and unable to command people's respect. (This particular concept is part of an overarching perspective that seeps throughout our whole culture, but that's another story.)

I should make it clear that if it makes your junk tingle to read about appalling specimens of humanity visiting adolescent viciousness on hapless victims, that's just fine. Read on and beat off. People's junk wants what it wants, and if that does it for you, I hope that you find equally excited partners with which to consensually explore a roller coaster of hideous BDSM scenes for your mutual fulfillment. I'm throwing no rocks in that glass house; I've certainly created fantasy scenarios to explore with willing partners that would make many people's eyes widen with shock or revulsion, and we all had a marvelous time. But by the time we make it to the breakfast table, another headspace has to come into play.

Reality is that as a leader, you'll be dealing with a lot of grievously mundane problems, and you will have to tackle them calmly and maturely. Handling your subordinates with skill and patience and understanding will be among those mundane problems, and those jobs must not be shirked. When you think that you don't have to earn mastery, but that it should just be handed to you on your say-so, you are bottoming to porn. When you believe that you've already done the initial slave-acquisition so you should now be able to slide by on your laurels, you are bottoming to porn. When you think that ordinary problems can be handled by condescendingly blowing off your subordinates (or by having kinky sex), you are bottoming to porn.

When your identification with a fictional version of your role prevents you from listening, or acknowledging a mistake, or talking about difficult things, or asking for help when you need it, or getting your vulnerable emotional needs met with this person who's supposed to give you what you want, you are bottoming to porn. Porn is in charge, not you—and porn, like the ego, is a good servant but a terrible master.

Another source of pressure which is even more of a mixed blessing is nonfiction books and articles by people who are actually practitioners, and the people themselves—often found at BDSM or M/s events, or online. I'm one of those writers, and I am glad of all the other books out there, because they helped me before I could find other human beings. I'm also glad of the live human beings I've listened to over the years; I'm a solid member of my MAsT group and I go to conferences where people I respect teach. I'm very much in favor of people using these resources, but it's important to keep perspective.

Each of us, all the authors and presenters, can only speak from our own experiences, and we have our own preferences and biases. It's all too easy for people who are just beginning to read one book, or listen to one person online, and decide that this is The Way It Should Be Done, and if that way turns out to be incompatible with the desires and practical life of both people in the relationship, one or both people may come to believe that they are not suited for this relationship style. This isn't uncommon—on some level, any of us with common sense know that this can be dangerous. We're playing with fire, and we have to learn skills and act correctly or someone will get burned. Some communities want—justifiably—to prevent unskilled people from making an ugly mess of things, so they lay out a way to do things, and tell everyone who comes in, "If you just do it this way you'll be safe."

The big problem comes when that way doesn't work for one or both of you. Actually, it's even harder when it works for one member of the couple but doesn't work for the other one, because at least if it's not right for either of you, you have each other to commiserate with and can encourage each other to try something else. When one person thinks it's just fine and the other one is profoundly uncomfortable, it's easy for the objector to believe that it's something wrong with them, and if they could just become a different person it would all be OK.

Many people would look at this situation and figure that it would only be a problem if it was the s-type who was the objector. That might be true if every person who decided they were going to be a master was suddenly flooded with automatic confidence in their every action, but in real life the reverse situation can make the beginning M-type very unsure of themselves, and they can go around in circles mentally.

We ran into this problem early on in our relationship. My slaveboy Joshua was enamored of gay leather protocols, had read everything on the subject, and assumed that because we were a same-sex couple we'd be using them. He figured I'd run my power dynamic by those rules. I had very little interest in those rules, that subculture, and that aesthetic; I wasn't sure at first what I wanted, but I knew it wasn't that. However, since he seemed to want it so much, I tried to do at least a little of it in order to make him happy. After all, a good master wants their slave to be happy, right?

But it just didn't work for me, and even with all my good intentions, if I wasn't feeling it, I would not be motivated to check and make sure he was doing the activity. (This linked into the other problem I discuss in my essay on Consistency.) If I wasn't personally invested in it—if it didn't touch me in some sincere way—it would just fall off my plate, no matter how hard I tried. Eventually I realized that we had to start over and create our own relationship style from scratch, figuring out what would work for both of us.

That felt a little scary, in the beginning—what if we couldn't find enough rules or rituals or mantras or acts of dominance and submission that worked for both of us? What if we couldn't find enough pieces to build a structure? That turned out to be a groundless fear, however. One tiny thing after another fell into place, and wove themselves together into a net to hold us. More than a decade later, we continue to find meaningful gestures that make both of us smile, small rituals that are in no one's book yet. For example, our most recent addition is that since I'm a crip and use a stair chair to ride upstairs—I call it my "flying throne"—the slaveboy is required to come out of his upstairs room when he hears the chair coming, and stand at the top of the stairs to greet me. It's not in any manual, but it reminds us who we are, and that we can make our own way that is special for us.

Another area where both porn and community standards seep in is sexual activities. Author Pat Califia once observed that if we study the porn, male dominants are allowed even fewer sexual activities (as opposed to kink activities) than what is socially accepted for straight vanilla guys—they can stick their dicks in things, and that's it. Everything else will supposedly damage their dominance. In reality, ethical and pleasant activities do not damage one's dominance, and indeed if you're really in charge, you should be able to get what you want, given everyone's physical limitations. If your s-type isn't sure how to do something, they can be trained to do it exactly the way you want.

However, we've had numerous M-types contact us and tell us that they wanted certain sexual activities that weren't in the limited porn-dominant menu, but they felt pressure both from the fictional models and—sadly enough—from community members who trumpeted loudly about how "real" dominant types wouldn't do those things. I'm appalled every time I hear that. Of all the relationship activities that we as co-residents of the Kingdom of Power Exchange should *not* be policing, I would say that sexual activities between the M-type and the s-type would be at the top of that list.

It's certainly easier to follow an existing model than to test thousands of possibilities. The problem is that you'll end up doing that anyway, as all the different rules you try to implement either grind to a halt or keep working. It's good to read the books (fiction or nonfiction) and listen to the people, but hold all these pieces lightly. Don't bet your relationship on any of them. The period we spent attempting gay leather rules wasn't entirely useless; we did retain perhaps five per cent of them and still find them useful. We also took another five per cent from that book, and another tidbit from this class, and patchworked it all together. You'll have to do that too, and the more you expose yourself to, the more pieces you'll have to pick from, and perhaps discard later. I promise you it's not that difficult. You probably already understand the process—it's how you figure out what you want out of life itself.

# Painting a Picture of Your Future:
# An Exercise for New Masters
*Carolyn*

Over several decades of talking with people both online and in person, one problem I see many new Doms and Masters mention is "How do I get started?" Or its less elegant derivation: "I got me a slave, so now what?" Well, it depends on where you want to go.

During the "How do I get started?" phase, one of the biggest mistakes I see among new Masters is focusing on feelings rather than behaviors. I love feelings—they are great. Saying "I am your Master, you are my slave!" to your partner makes you both feel terrific. But what does it mean? "Oh, it means I'm his to use as he wishes" says Miss Slave. But what does *that* mean? "Oh, it means she has surrendered to me totally," says Mr. Master. Like I said, what does that mean?

This exercise is about painting a picture in your mind of what the relationship you want to create looks like. And it's about the first steps in creating that new, wonderful and exciting reality. It's about finding out where you want to go.

But it assumes some things up front.

## *Some Background*

First, to avoid using Dom or Master, or D-type etc. I will use the terms Master and slave, but it applies to all labels for a fairly extensive authority transfer relationship. I also don't like to use plural pronouns for a single person, or the long-winded "he or she". So, I will use he and him for the Master and she or her for the slave. If you can't live with that, please skip this article.

Second, I am of the belief that the Master needs to have a picture of what he wants his M/s relationship to look like. I think a smart Master is flexible and adjusts the picture for the reality of life and his partner. But this exercise assumes that knowing where you as a Master want to go is important to you.

If you are a "let it evolve naturally" person, you may not be able to get into this exercise. Give it a try. No one is going to hold you to anything. But a basic assumption here is that Masters both want to, and need to know where they are going.

Third this article is geared towards either a total authority transfer dynamic or at least something close to that in which one Master is in charge of the slave's life well beyond kinky play and sex.

This exercise is for people who want to take on the responsibility of being what used to be called Head of Household—the person who says "the buck stops here" when it comes to your relationship.

With that background, if you're still game, let's start.

## Creating Your Picture

Set aside an hour or two when you can be alone and will not be interrupted. Find yourself a comfortable, quiet and private spot to sit. Bring along your favorite adult beverage and perhaps put on some thinking music, if you have such a thing. Close your eyes and picture a perfect, but perfectly normal weekday, two years from now. Picture how you'd like things to be.

*Wait!* Back up. Don't picture yourself in a medieval castle unless you actually live in one or can reasonably buy one in the next year or so. Don't picture the two of you playing kinky games 24/7 unless you are independently wealthy and have lots of energy. No fair having won a lottery in the intervening two years. Make it realistic.

But if you have a partner already, assume she is magically totally ready, willing, and able to step into the picture without discord. If you don't have a partner, assume you will find one, equally ready willing and able to stop into the picture. This part of the exercise is about what you realistically want, without regard (just yet) for your partner. We'll add the partners in later.

I realize this is difficult if you have a partner already. But I believe knowing what *you* want will ultimately lead to a happier and longer lasting relationship. Masters do compromise, but it helps to know what your starting point is.

OK, back to picturing the perfect but normal weekday. How does it start? Do you get up before your partner and rush off to work? Are your clothes laid out for you? Has the coffee pot been set to start on time? Who did that? Does your partner get up first and make you a full breakfast? Do you start the day with sex? Do you have it in bed or in the shower? You're creating your fantasy day, so go for it.

How busy are you at work? It may *feel* great for your slave to have to ask for permission to pee, but does your job permit you time to get and answer texts all day? So maybe your fantasy has you in a different job. That's fair. It's your fantasy. But if your slave is a surgeon, it's not realistic to have her call you to ask permission to pee, unless she changes her job. That's what I mean by realistic.

Go through this perfect but normal weekday slowly and in detail. Focus on what happens, not how you feel, because the assumption is you feel good and happy about it. It's perfect.

Once you've gotten your picture of a perfect but perfectly normal day then stand up, walk around a bit. Maybe take a cold shower too. Then sit down again.

### Checking For Reality

Go over your perfect but perfectly normal weekday with a critical eye as to what is realistic or not. Again, you're assuming your partner will love the picture you are painting. Other than that, don't make changes you can't control. Make sure you didn't slip in some totally undoable things. Days will still have 24 hours in two years. You will still have to pee and take a crap (this isn't an episode of *Star Trek* where the Enterprise doesn't need bathrooms). Traffic has not been eliminated in two years, so allow time for that. You still need to eat and probably someone needs to prepare food.

When you thought about starting the day with sex, did your picture included prolonged, pounding sex? If so, have you left enough time for that, given that you may also have pictured prolonged play at night? Did your picture allow time for your slave to recover and make you a three-course breakfast? Maybe your picture should have you having a quickie in the morning, not that long scene with bondage, flogging and four orgasms for your slave.

Your picture of a perfect but perfectly normal weekday could include changes you can control. You could change your job. You could move (please tell me you didn't picture your perfect day in your mother's basement, did you)?

When you're done, you'll have a picture of your perfect but realistic future. But it's with someone, right, so let's talk about that very important part of the picture, and then I'll talk about getting from today to bringing life to the picture you painted.

### Adding an Existing Partner

OK, now we stop the mental masturbation and add in a partner. If you have a partner, talk to your partner and see what she expects from your relationship. Maybe you can tell your slave to do the exercise for themselves, but you could also just ask them to describe their vision of a perfect but perfectly normal day two years in the future. Do this before you share your picture, because your slave might just accept that as a done deal, and you really do want to know what she pictures. So ask her for that.

*Wait!* I can hear her answer already. "Whatever you want it to look like, Master." Or "That's not my job—you are supposed to design our future." Here's a clue. Sometimes getting preferences from a slave is difficult. How to do it is beyond the scope of this article, but I'll give you some clues. First: Some (but not that many) people honestly have no idea what they want for the future. You job as Master is to figure out if this is the case with your slave. However, many slaves are so focused on Master when they are new that they are either afraid to express their hopes and wishes, or they think they shouldn't do so.

Clue number two is that you might need to explain that you need information to make the best decisions for you both. You may require that the slave provide you with the information about how the slave would like the future to look. And finally, let the slave know that you will take her vision, along with your vision, and create a path.

Once you hear your slave's vision, see how it aligns with the picture you created. Since the vision isn't written in stone, getting close is enough to move forward. You can and will adjust as you go, and things outside of your control will happen to modify your picture a little here and there.

If your pictures aren't too far off, share yours with her. If your pictures are very different, well … you've learned something important. You need to have a long talk with your slave. Hard as that may be, it's better to do it now, than in five or ten years.

## No Partner, No Problem

If you don't have a partner yet, you don't have to worry about having that long talk about how you both have different visions of the future. You're lucky; you can use your picture as a "finding a partner" tool. Paint your picture, perhaps in less detail, in words that someone else can read. Don't make it just about you, add in your dream partner. Use this to show a potential partner what you want, and to see if you and she are compatible.

But if you don't have a partner, don't get too wedded to anything in your picture of the perfect relationship, because it will change when you do have a partner. It can, however, be a tool in screening a potential partner.

## Now What?

Here's the big next step, which is still useful for those without a partner as well as those with one. Look at the picture you created. What's different now from that future picture? For example, are you not living together? Well, that may have to change if your picture has you both in the same house. Put it on the "has to change" list. Does your day in the future start with a blow job, but right now your slave gags on even shallow oral sex? Put "blow job training" on the list. Go through your day and literally make a list of what has to change to get to that perfect but perfectly normal weekday. Don't forget the non-kinky things. Do you spend three hours commuting, which would make your dream life undoable? Well, it's time to start thinking about how to change that.

Now talk to your slave. Ask her what she thinks is needed to change today into your vision of a perfect but perfectly normal weekday. Maybe she'll notice some things about you that would need to change too. If your slave is the better logistics organizer between the two of you, have her help, or have her make the first round of lists.

Then prioritize things, not only by what's most important to you, but what will take the longest and be the most difficult to change. Break that down into steps. Again, use your slave's skills to help you with this. It is equivalent to a manager creating a work-flow chart for a complex project.

*Wait!* Yes, I hear you screaming *"Wait!"* again. This isn't what you thought being a Master was about! You thought it was about getting blow jobs whenever you want, and never having to get up to get a beer again in your life. OK, Sparky, that's not my idea of an M/s relationship. I said up-front that this was about taking responsibility for another person's life. Did you think that would happen magically with no effort on your part? Well, you're wrong. So perhaps this is a good time to think about whether you have the focus, time, self-control, and commitment—and are willing to put in the effort—to create and sustain an M/s relationship. There's nothing wrong with just plain kinky fun-times and someone calling you Master during a scene, and if that's what you want, great. However, that's not what this article is about.

But if you didn't scream out in pain over the idea of actually making a list of what needs to change to get from today to your perfect but perfectly normal weekday two years from now—congratulations! You've taken two huge steps towards a wonderful life. You've painted a picture of your future, and you've made a list of what needs to change to get there. You've answered the question "How do I get started?" and your goals came from *your* vision of your future self, so you are likely to actually want to take the steps necessary to create your new and wonderful reality.

So now I suggest you give yourself and your slave a little reward. Find something on the "needs to change" list that would be fun to implement. Maybe work on that "greeting me when I come home" ritual or the gag reflex. If you're alone, maybe put up that fence that will allow you to have sex in the back yard with no one watching. Start having fun with your changes. But don't forget the bigger ones: moving in together or changing jobs or whatever. Don't let those wait until it's a year and eleven months from now. Start the plan and make it happen.

*Carolyn was a late bloomer. OK, enough with the third party. I hid my leanings in the kinky direction even from myself. To my total surprise, an inner dominant burst forth when I was in my 40s, and a new boyfriend*

*confessed his interest in "dominant women". I raced off to an adult bookstore, bought SM101 and Different Loving, and through the latter found the D/s section in the Human Sexuality Forum on CompuServe where I eventually became a "section leader."*

*That was then, now I'm 23 years into a TAT (total authority transfer) relationship with a guy I met on CompuServe. I had said, in a discussion, I wanted to live in a 1950s TV sitcom with one head of household, lots of love and laughter, but with the genders reversed. A nice, funny, intelligent guy said that sounded perfect, and then went off to become someone else's sub. But he eventually worked his way around to me.*

*We now live in rural Texas, in a happy and loving home where I'm the head of household and my husband ... well he's not Mary Tyler Moore in capri pants. But he's the best first mate I could possibly want.*

# Negotiation

*Mistress Sky*

Here you are, standing next to your special somebody who already hangs on your every word. You both feel so fortunate to have found each other. Now what you need is a system—your own unique system—to support your shiny new relationship's continuous good health. It's time to do the business of relationship and together you can get the job done. Your unequal relationship foundation begins with negotiation. You and your partner(s) will use negotiation to learn about each other. You will:

❖ Identify what is most important to each of you (needs).
❖ Learn the difference between needs and desires.
❖ Understand your role as dominant/leading partner in negotiations.
❖ Realize how much power and control you want to be responsible for.
❖ Decide on specific issues to negotiate.
❖ Learn how to create a relationship contract.

This is how you make your first agreements when you and your partner(s) are going forward. Negotiating will give you your truth about whether or not you should form a committed relationship. Negotiating is crucial—it's the reasonable start that I would wish for you and yours. I want to give you thinking points for designing your own negotiation protocols so that your unequal relationship has the best chance of succeeding.

## What Can You Expect from Negotiating?

Are the results a commitment like a marriage license? Is it a promise to proceed—i.e. the s-type is now your consensually-appointed property or, at least, your submissive or slave? No. No. And no. I want you to be clear about the purpose of negotiations. *Negotiations are never, ever a guarantee of partnership or of having a future together.* Maybe you will or maybe you won't go on to create an unequal relationship. Negotiations will be a proofing space as to *whether* you should go forward with your person or not.

First, whatever is learned throughout negotiations is a blessing, because it's the truth. You and your partner(s) are winners no matter if your truth is to go forward as master and s-type or to let each other go. Prospective unequal partners have been known to let unequal partnership go because that was their truth, but transitioned into different relationship roles with each other.

Second, *you can expect to have a set of agreements that will govern how you and your partners will relate to each other and how exactly you will proceed in order to meet your combined needs.* That container of agreements forms an exoskeleton for your relationship. You're going to discover that decision-making is much easier once the Big Picture items have been discussed and agreements have been made.

### Is it a Need or Is it a Desire?

When I speak to audiences, I quickly dive into my explanation of the startling difference between corporate culture's negotiating business and negotiating unequal relationship business in one's personal life. This is what I tell them:

❖ **Business or Corporate:** Business partners stand in opposition. Each person has an intention of getting all they can to benefit themselves. No one feels any responsibility for the other person's interests. Business negotiations may take place amicably, but there is nothing that says either party has to care about the other.

❖ **Personal:** In personal negotiations, partners are invested in the happiness and well-being of the other(s). In fact, you enter negotiations with the primary notion of satisfying your partner's needs. Your partner or partners are doing the same. You set the intention of leaving behind the negative energy of worrying that your needs aren't going to get met, and then you schedule a series of discussions. You and the partner(s) delight in discovering what your individual needs are. *You are learning how to work together in this discovery.* You'll learn how to work collaboratively even more by tackling how you can satisfy your combined needs.

Next, you and I must talk about the difference between *desires* and *needs*. Did you notice that so far I've repeatedly referenced "needs"?

Needs are the business of negotiations between unequal partners. Your love of tea and scones might be a preference, but is it essential to your life? Your sweet tooth or your desire to eat meat are preferences. What time to serve lunch or dinner is probably a preference. But if scheduling precision is crucial to your mental/emotional stability, then it deserves a place in negotiation discussions. So it is *needs* that we must get to. What is it that you feel that you cannot live without? My list includes knowledge of and respect for my dietary restrictions, my polyamorous practices which means the possibility of having other partners, my spiritual practices which directly influence life with my partners, my sexual practices, my need to sleep alone, and my need to *not* live together. (My submissive life partner had a unique list of needs to add to mine.) You can tell the difference between wants and needs if you compare my needs list to my wants list. My wants list includes my fondness for sandwiches with mayo, fruit pies, silk or super-soft-cotton bed sheets, international travel, biking and hiking with my sub. Understand?

### Your Leadership Role

During negotiation it is already time for the leader to lead. Well, time to lead, yes, but not to dictate terms. That's because your prospective partner is still a totally free agent who can choose to enter into this relationship or not. You have the great responsibility of making sure that true consent for each of you is honored today and every day going forward. They can accept what you are offering, or ask for modifications, or none of the above. They are free to ask questions and expect useful, honest answers. They can and will have their own ideas for how the relationship should be formed and what they expect to gain.

Leadership at this point also looks like monitoring the comfort level of your person. Try to keep all conditions comfortable for you both or true consent might erode. Does he/she/they feel free to speak? How able are they to give voice to their needs? How can you be encouraging and open? Those are the questions to keep in mind.

❖ *A dominant/leading partner is always accountable to the other unequal partner(s).*

❖ A dominant/leading partner *always claims responsibility for their own actions.*

❖ A dominant/leading partner *always behaves honorably.*

Make sure that your prospective sub or slave knows that there is no commitment during the negotiation process. Commitment is purely each individual's choice, which may or may not result from negotiating. True Consent is not a one-time thing. Consent, yours and your partner's, is an on-going re-commitment until it is negated, which is to say that either partner can withdraw consent at any time. An honest dominant/leading partner/head of household makes this very clear during negotiations and re-negotiations.

The dominant/leading partner must have pretty good control over his/her/their emotions. No one is asking you to be constantly stoic, and in no way should you be denying your feelings. But you can commit to a reasonable expression of feelings, moderating how you express yourself, taking a deep breath and giving your s-type the benefit of the doubt instead of jumping into an emotional display of any kind. Take a step back from the situation as needed. Don't think that you must respond immediately. Give yourself time to lead with higher consciousness rather than lower emotions before, during, and after negotiating.

Check over your inner landscape. Make sure you're ready to be a kind, open-hearted and open-minded leading partner. Are you able to be fully present and really listen? Are you ready to negotiate? When was the last time that you took alone time to refresh and renew? Regular self-care is a requirement for your good health.

I once knew a male dominant from Nova Scotia who had forgotten to prioritize self-care. His existence had become totally about taking care of his unequal partner and their children and his other mates, plus all of his volunteerism in the community. The consequences included muddled thinking, second-guessing himself, loneliness, and anguish. My prescription for him was regular self-care in the form of yoga, a team sport, quiet reading time, walking, and meditation. He said, "I used to do those things." Yeah, well, add them back onto the calendar.

*Owning your own story is the bravest thing we'll ever do.*

–Brené Brown, author and inspirational speaker

Practice having inner dialogues about who you want to be as the leading partner in an unequal partnership. For instance, some dominants want to be known, most especially, as a protector for their slave. A protector might be kind, romantic, and snuggly-emotional with their s-type, or a protector might carry a bold warrior persona with a bit of emotional distance added for good measure. The snuggly emotional one exudes the great warmth that is very important to some dominants and some s-types. The bold warrior persona is probably based on a strong need to be held in high esteem by the sub or slave. Another dominance style might be based on intellectualism and the submissive's admiration of her master's big brain. Another might be based on spirituality and the sub's reverence of the master/guru. Spirituality could also look like service to the master as the only representative of the submissive's sacred connection to a Higher Power. There are numerous mind pictures and archetypes of what it means to be the master. Reading these few, what image comes to mind for your dominance style? What character traits strike you as most important and very comfortable for your personality?

It is best not to equate being a relationship dominant with assuming an acting role. You want to build your dominance style based on the Real You. That's the only path that is sustainable in a relationship (as opposed to a play scene). It is your authentic being that you want to offer your partner in a real unequal relationship that will benefit you both. Discuss whatever you have realized about your dominance style with your prospective partner(s). Going forward, let self-awareness drive your communication with your s-type so that they come to know the Real You.

### How Much Power and Control Do You Want Responsibility For?

Decide on how much power and control you ultimately want even if ideally you and your partner start with only a few areas to give you control over. Discuss both the starter set of control transfer and, separately, how much you'd really like to have in the future if there is a difference. Don't ask for control over areas that are not important to you. You may feel crazy-enthusiastic about having control over everything, but think seriously about the impact on *your* life if you quickly gobble up too much.

So how much power and control should you take responsibility for? It depends. It can depend on how each of you feels about giving up control/accepting control in a particular area. Let your feelings be your measuring instrument, and then be supportive of each other no matter where the Gut Gauge leads you.

As an example, Marin is a master who considers herself to be an equity and inclusivity activist and as such doesn't feel completely comfortable assuming responsibility for her slave's finances. The slave counts themselves as a feminist and as such had argued against handing over control of financial assets to their master. That is, the slave fought the idea until they realized that "I never in my life enjoyed numbers and taking care of my own finances. So, why was I fighting to hold on to control over an area that I did not care about?"

### Time to Set the Right Tone and to Begin Negotiating

The leading unequal partner must take responsibility for setting the right tone for negotiations. You want to do everything that you can think of to create a loving, open-minded, welcoming, and truly consensual environment for yourself and your partner. Suggest some lovely and comfortable location for your discussions. My partner and I have always chosen natural settings like mountain hiking trails, a scenic path along a long city canal, my wonderful backyard. Hint: Never do relationship business or job tasks in the bedroom. Leave your bedroom as sacred space, as relaxation space, like a spa. No television!

Okay, so now, you and the partner(s) are meeting at your chosen location. Everything feels great. Ask: If you could have anything, what would be a deep, heart-centered relationship wish? Here are ideas to stir your thoughts:

❖ Stability
❖ Love, romance
❖ A deep emotional bond without romantic love
❖ Trust
❖ Commitment

- ❖ Service
- ❖ Something lasting
- ❖ Dominance within a deeply meaningful relationship because that's who I am
- ❖ Submission within a deeply meaningful relationship because that's who I am
- ❖ Partnership, partnering long-term
- ❖ A nesting arrangement (we live together)
- ❖ Commitment but not living together
- ❖ Further personal growth, self-development
- ❖ Support for where I want to grow professionally
- ❖ A trustworthy relationship structure for raising children
- ❖ A trustworthy relationship structure without children

### What Do You Need to Negotiate?

In the past, I gave a talk about negotiating to a roomful of sex therapists. They immediately looked confused. They asked, "What is there to negotiate?" I hope that you will seek them out and tell them that the correct answer is "Everything!" Well, *potentially* everything, since what gets negotiated is up to you and your partner(s). I am going to give you some ideas, but the best starting point is to expect to negotiate whatever is most important to you and your partners. That's the reason that negotiations in your household will never be the same as what I am doing with my partners. Your agreements will be unique to your combined needs. *Negotiating is a mutually respectful process for revealing major needs of each partner and creating agreements for how best to meet those needs.*

What do you need to negotiate? Here are some Big Picture possibilities that you might consider for your negotiations. Design your lists based on needs and what is most important:

- ❖ Where we want to live.

- ❖ Whether we want to live together (because we don't have to).

- ❖ What tasks are worth paying others to do (which is the same as asking ourselves about the priorities for use of our time together).

- ❖ Whether we will socialize together.

❖ Whether each of us will socialize with others; are there limits and if so, why?

❖ Protocols regarding how we behave in public as a couple.

❖ Monogamy versus non-monogamy versus polyamory versus an open relationship.

❖ Having a relationship that includes sex versus a relationship without sex. Terms for having sex and what kind of sex.

❖ Play sessions; how much play and when.

❖ What do you, as dominant, intend to provide? Some type of training, perhaps? Emotional support? Financial support? Life coaching? Really phenomenal sex? Regular play sessions? What do you never intend to provide? What might you expect to provide over time?

❖ What are your thoughts about dealing with feelings and showing vulnerability? Do you, the dominant, expect to be involved with your s-type's inner life? Are you going to share deeply and be vulnerable with your special person? Whatever your answers are be honest with your s-type.

❖ Finances are a Big Picture item even if you do not intend to live together. Who will pay for dinners out or tickets to a concert should be discussed. Finances include a question of whether you, the dominant, have any control over the other person's assets (bank accounts, future income, land, houses, businesses, and other holdings). What about inheritance? Don't be surprised if your prospective partner does not grant you access to any of their wealth besides contributing to daily costs (like being roommates). However, the partner may go the other way and ask your opinions and agree to whatever you think best for the two of you. If you jointly decide that all or some part of the partner's income is under your control then you absolutely must think very carefully about their care—and that means their care today and their care tomorrow, in the case of a breakup or any other reason where the partner would be on their own. Some dominants create a bank account in the partner's name and arrange for regular contributions to it.

❖ Dealing with the partner's relatives can be a complicated scenario. Derive your plan together with agreements about power and control. In some households the partner makes his/her own decisions about contact with family, caretaking of relatives, and financial contributions to relatives, and the agreement is merely the partner's pledge to keep the dominant partner informed about his/her/their time, etc. If there are situations that the dominant judges to be potentially harmful, and judges the partner to be unable to extricate themselves or to defend their own personal space, then sometimes—with the partner's full consent—the dominant makes very strong directives limiting how involved the two of you will be with the relatives.

Remind yourself now and throughout these discussions that you and your partner are fondly discovering each other. You can and should encourage both of you to toss your ideals on the table. Play a vigorous game of We Can Have Anything We Want. Don't be afraid of posing the question, "Why are we together?" Use your ideals about the relationship, and ideals about what you want in life as a whole, to answer, "What is the purpose of our relationship?" Just as businesspeople devise plans and a statement of purpose for their business, you and your partner(s) can imagine purpose for yourselves together. This will take some envisioning and trusting yourselves to hear your truth. You want to listen for the deepest reasons for what your relationship can be expected to support. I urge you to read through the lists in this article again and again. You might find your answers or be brain-sparked with a whole new idea.

Of course, there is a bit more to take seriously in your negotiations. These are Things to Handle Carefully:

❖ Medical issues and health concerns.
❖ Nutritional needs and/or restrictions.
❖ Responsibility for existing children.
❖ Responsibility for existing commitments, professional and personal.
❖ Caretaking of parents or other relatives.

Honoring previous commitments could mean no transfer of control over job responsibilities or over business ownership and business management. Personal commitments could include other relationships and other partners.

### Having It All Via Your Agreements

"Everything" is out on the table. So, now, switch mental gears so that whatever you see before you are your *combined needs*. Discuss one by one how each need can be dealt with. What conditions will work best for you both? Which matters can be directly handled by one of you, or should be dealt with by both of you? Learn to recognize when certain needs are best met outside of your relationship, such as medical care, education for one of you or for children, or mental health support. These are the most exhilarating discussions for unequal partners. You are literally sculpting your shared life together through forging your first set of agreements.

Having come this far in your shared understanding about your relationship future, you might want to have a discussion about relationship goals. Ask the question, "What goals do we have together at this time?" Hold onto that question for later in the relationship, too. A dominant/leading partner monitors how well the partners are doing in achieving their goals—what's going well and what needs either modification or a whole new plan for achieving success. This work goes a very long way toward creating your lasting bond.

It's also possible that your sincere work may show you that unequal partnership is not for you. At this point, it's time to commit to each other going forward as an unequal partnership, to switch to negotiating an egalitarian relationship, or to let go of each other with kindness.

### Relationship Contracts

*Write down your agreements.* For some unequal partners a single sheet of paper says it all. For others, after several or many discussions, their agreements take up much more space. Your agreements in writing constitute your relationship contract. One unequal couple that I know created a poster-sized print of their agreements and included it in their wedding ceremony, and the guests signed it as witnesses. A relationship contract is not legally binding, but between or among unequal partners it is a sacred document that is precious. Consider including a statement that acknowledges each partner's right to initiate re-negotiation, and that the request will be honored immediately or within a reasonable amount of time.

Your relationship contract must:

❖ Represent a truly consensual relationship between you and your partner(s).
❖ Refer to a limited time period, which is explicitly stated. The contract can be renewed.
❖ Include an exit clause.

The exit clause is an important part of establishing true consent. "You are free today and in this moment, and you are free every day." "No one has any right to hold you as chattel or to force you to do anything. You are free." "I freely enter into these agreements with you." If the healthy, wholesome time for your relationship comes to an end, be honest, be compassionate, and be kind to each other as you let the relationship go. Make good short-term plans for the post-relationship welfare of each of you. Include in the relationship contract a couple of sentences about what each of you would like to happen if you must take care of each other at the end of your relationship. I have asked conference audiences to imagine what would be kind in their opinion and this is what they said:

❖ "I'd want our ending to happen over a series of discussions, not one abrupt conversation."
❖ "I'd like an agreement that nothing is posted in social media about our private life together."
❖ "I would want my partner to be honest with me. No secrets or starting a new life without ending our relationship first."
❖ "I would want our finances to be kept separately so that there can be no arguments over money if we ever ended."

My last word about why we include an exit clause has to do with respect. If you regarded each other highly at the beginning of the relationship, and if you held each other in high regard throughout a significant time in your lives, how can you do any differently if you must end the relationship? Be kind. Be gracious and wish each other well.

Remember that neither of you is agreeing to anything that cannot be renegotiated. Your agreements are fluid and can be modified. Your life together will be conducted within the influence of those agreements. Everyday decision-making is so much easier if done within the context of your Big Picture agreements. The agreements were created by you, together, and are to be adhered to honorably by each of you. You, the dominant/leading partner, will have done your job to this point admirably by leading both of you through negotiations. The strength and beauty of negotiating will shine throughout your partnership.

# What You Want and What You Can Have (And What to Do When That's Not So Clear)
*Raven Kaldera*

The title sums it up: Understanding and balancing the above two points will be one of the hardest things you do in the beginning phase of mastery. Except that sometimes it sounds easier in theory that it actually is in practice.

### First: What You Want

You may come into this journey with a lot of ideas about what you want out of this experience. I can tell you right now that a significant percentage of those ideas will end up being thrown by the wayside. That's not failure, it's just calibration. Think of this relationship as a garden you are cultivating, in a new place where you're not sure of the climate or rainfall or, in the case of a new relationship, the basic soil you'll be growing in. Some seeds won't come up, some plants may grow for a little while but will not be sustainable enough to survive the cold winters or hot summers. After a couple of years, you'll have figured out what will live and grow, and you'll focus on those. So let's start with planning the garden, as it were, with the assumption that there's going to be a necessary attrition rate.

Start by writing down what you already think you want. I suggest making a "macro" list and a "micro" list. The "macro" list should be large overall subjects, like "Housework" or "Personal Body Service" or "Sex" or "Romantic/Non-Romantic". The "micro" list can just be a brain-dump of secondary and tertiary activities or situations under that, like "I want my hair brushed every morning" or "I want someone who will play World of Warcraft with me". This step can be done even if you don't have a partner yet. However, there's only so far you can go with this.

The second step is to figure out what you don't know yet that you want. This is especially an issue for people who have been raised to deny their desires—perhaps the family was poverty-stricken or dysfunctional, and the children had to put their own desires or even their needs aside in order to cope with damaged parents. Women are especially prone to this, as they are more often expected to defer to others rather than asserting or even finding out what they want, but men are not immune either. I've anecdotally seen a higher percentage of oldest children in the M-type demographic, but in a dysfunctional family the oldest child of either gender is often expected to take care of everyone else's needs, including that of the parents.

This doesn't necessarily lead to a compliant and submissive personality. The I-must-take-care-of-everyone person can also be dominant and fiercely independent; taking care of others can become a way of gaining power in the situation, not to mention avoiding depending on possibly untrustworthy people for one's own emotional survival. Such individuals may end up "rescuer" types, taking on high-maintenance partners whose needs, of course, eat up everyone's attention. (This can be disastrous for an M-type, but that's a different conversation.) The side effect of this kind of complex is that the would-be M-type has very little idea what would actually make them happy. If they are one of those dominant and fiercely independent types, the last thing they want is to admit that they don't know.

If I sound like my knowledge of this path is pretty comprehensive, you're right. I don't have a submissive bone in my body, but I grew up being told, "You can't have it, so don't bother to ask." That didn't just go for toys, it also applied to such things as my physical and emotional safety. As a dominant, I went through a series of submissive types. I asked them what they were willing to give, chose what I liked from that menu, and never mentioned my own needs, or even many of my desires. (Showing that I had needs would make me vulnerable, or so I thought.) Specifically, I didn't bring up the ones that meant the most to me, the ones that would really wound me to have rejected, or—even worse—promised and then not given. *You can't have it, so don't bother to ask.*

Then I got myself a real slave for the first time—someone who would look me in the eye and say, "I want to give you as much as I can of what you're not getting. I want to be a place where you can be selfish. I want to make your life easier in any way that is possible for me." I wanted very badly to trust him, but trusting anyone was excruciating for me. Besides, there was that issue about not knowing what would make me happy or make my life easier, because I hadn't ever expected anyone else to make me happy, and I didn't know what that would look like. It also hadn't occurred to me that my life could really be made easier, because I was used to it being hard.

Most of you won't be going into mastery with this kind of a handicap. If so, you can skip this part. But a certain percentage of you will, and you're who I'm talking to right now. You know who you are. You might feel uncomfortable when asked to imagine your perfect life, because that's been entirely off your radar until now. You may have plenty of ideas in your head about things you might want because they sound like fun, but the things that will make you deeply happy may be largely an undiscovered country.

While that may be somewhat embarrassing to admit, exploring those needs and desires is an adventure worth having. However, it's very difficult to start until you actually have an s-type to help you. I had to start by experimenting, and it was important to tell my early-days slave that these were actually just experiments and they might not work out. S-types can take it pretty personally if they throw themselves into an activity and it doesn't make you happy, so when you start trying things out, it's important to warn them that it's not their fault in any way if it doesn't work for you. Let them know that the service they're rendering to you is helping you with the experiment in general, and as long as they're doing their best on whatever you come up with, you're satisfied with their performance. This takes the pressure off the specific activity and puts it onto the adventure itself, where the two of you are partners in the search.

If you venture onto a quest to figure out what makes things better for you and what doesn't do the job, taking the s-type's suggestions into account is something to be used carefully. It can be very positive, as it communicates to them that you see them as a smart, perceptive, creative resource—and if they are those things, it's a shame not to use them as such—but you have to be careful to examine every suggestion to see how you feel about it. They might be enthusiastic about the idea, and *really sure* that you'd like it if you just tried it … but the second you give in and go along with their enthusiasm just to make them happy, you have lost the reins in the relationship. There are plenty of small, inconsequential areas where you can indulge your s-type when they want to try something together. This is not one of them. Your search needs to be you-driven, or it risks falling back into those old patterns of ignoring the question. Take on new power exchange activities *only* if they appeal to *you*.

If you're partnerless, much of the process will have to wait until later. However, there are still a few ways you can look into it, starting with talking to other power exchange people. Ask them about the parts of the relationship that make them deeply happy, and think about whether to add that to your lists. (I would also suggest reading plenty of books on the topic, which are listed in the appendix at the back. I'd especially suggest *Real Service* and *Negotiating Your Power Dynamic Relationship*.)

Before we move on, I want to point out one very important question that you might not have considered yet. *What items are necessary to you feeling like you're actually in charge?* Those are your deal-breakers, at least in terms of a power dynamic relationship as opposed to an egalitarian one. Every M-type has an emotional line drawn in the sand, and if they have to step beyond it, they no longer feel as if they are actually the authority in the relationship; the title seems meaningless at that point. Those points will be highly personal, extremely varied from M-type to M-type, and completely irrational. One M-type won't feel in charge unless they have a stay-at-home partner, or at least can make them quit their job; another won't mind at all if the s-type has a career. One won't feel like a master unless they can alter the s-type's look and style; another won't really care about that. One won't take on an s-type bringing in a child from a former relationship unless they have full parental authority; another will just shrug philosophically and say that it's not important. It doesn't matter so much where your line is so much as that you know it intimately and are very honest about it. Drawing it too far back can get you into a relationship where you're winsomely told that you're in charge, but you're just not feeling it, which is a sad and unsustainable place to be.

*Second: What You Can Have*

Now we move to the issue of what you can have. Any of the items on your list might eventually have to come off it, for any of the following reasons:

1) After you try it, you realize that it isn't as enjoyable as you thought it would be. This happens a lot with kinky sex activities, which sound all kinds of sexy in porn or in fantasy but sometimes just don't measure up in real life. However, it can also apply to any number of everyday services or responsibilities as well.

2) It's enjoyable, but it ends up requiring so much work and effort on your part, or your slave's part, or both your parts, that on balance it's not really worth it.

3) It doesn't work for your real life. This doesn't just apply to crazy scenarios you'd have to be ridiculously wealthy to pull off. It could seem like it ought to work, but end up being impractical for reasons that weren't apparent at first.

4) It could work for a while, and then something changed regarding your external circumstances, and now it is being sabotaged by outside problems you can't necessarily do away with. For example, your slave used to walk around naked and in chains, but now you've got kids or an aging parent living with you and that's off the table.

5) It might be something your s-type just can't offer for whatever reason. (Or they were once able to offer it, but can't do it now, perhaps due to the aforementioned unexpected life circumstances—for example, they have developed arthritis and can no longer kneel.)

Maybe you'll find out What You Can't Have during the negotiation phase. That's actually the best time to figure it out, because the two of you are not yet deeply invested, and can either back off from each other, or back off from the idea of a power dynamic. It's harder when you figure it out a good way into the relationship, and especially so if you hit it during the abovementioned experiments in figuring out what you want. It's hardest of all when it's something that worked for a time and then stopped working due to external issues you can't control.

Either way, one of the hardest parts of your job is looking at What You Can't Have and accepting it maturely. Being mature about it includes the following:

❖ Not blaming. Skip blame and go directly to problem-solving. If no solutions turn up, turn the problem-solving on yourself and ask, "Is there a way I can cope without this thing and still be happy? Can I find an alternative that gives me the same joy, or just focus on what I can have and be grateful for that?"

❖ Not whining. If it's painful, it's OK to calmly say that once or twice, but there's no point in continually bringing it up. You'll be setting an example for your s-type to follow of courageously moving on with life. If the s-type is also sad about it, it's OK to occasionally commiserate, so long as it's framed as a mutual loss you can both comfort each other about.

❖ Not blowing up at your s-type over it. That never helps, especially if it's because they can't give it to you. Losing control of yourself is not a dominant behavior. (On the other hand, being able to bravely express your feelings is a sign of strength.) Your job is to pull things together, not to make them worse.

❖ Not trying to force the issue and attempt to get what you want in the face of "No!" This can be done with intimidation, or manipulation, or trying to wear the partner down with repeated pushing. Don't go there. It dishonors your position and will eventually wreck your credibility.

❖ Not going into a negative spiral where you decide that this whole power dynamic thing is futile and stupid. (If you're the sort who is prone to this, you know who you are.)

❖ If you're the sort of person I was speaking to earlier in the article who has a history of being made to deny your needs, don't let this push you back into "I probably can't have anything I want, so why bother to ask?" This may be painful, but it's important to fight back the temptation to fall back down that well. If you need to take a trust break for a bit, go ahead, but it will be worth your while to keep trying to trust and explore if it's at all possible.

❖ Most importantly, if you find that you can't have the things that make you feel like you're in charge—if the limitations in the situation push you beyond that line—don't give up and pretend you believe you're still the leader while you're not feeling it's really true. That is a betrayal of yourself and your dominant soul, and you won't be able to keep it up for long anyway. You'll start pulling away and avoiding your responsibilities, and probably your partner as well. Don't do it. Instead, take a deep breath and set boundaries. A boundary is not a rule. A rule is "You (or I, or we) must do this." A boundary is "I refuse to do that." If you can't have what you need to feel like you're really the leader, refuse to go further with the power dynamic, whatever that entails. Don't compromise on this, no matter how upset the s-type is. If you don't get those needs met, the power dynamic cannot survive. You need to have compassion for yourself as well. Remember that you also have the right to set limits on what you will endure, and to vote with your feet and walk out if necessary.

It may take several years to create your final list, and Life tends to throw us enough curve balls that we need to be flexible. The balance of What You Want and What You Can Have is a constant shifting dance, with (fortunately for our sanity) periods of settling in and becoming used to each New Normal. The integrity of an M-type is shown by how sensibly they can handle that dance, neither erring in the direction of over-aggressiveness or self-sacrifice. If you're wincing to think about it, I've got one bright spot to light your way, after almost two decades of a deep power dynamic: It gets easier. The more you do the dance, the more you breathe and do the mature thing, the more skilled you will become at handling the hard parts in a fair and balanced way. That's why it's important to start now.

# The Wisdom to Change: Can You? Should You?
*Master Jim*

My advice to my past self as a Master just starting out would include the partial quote "... grant me the serenity to accept the things I cannot change, the courage to change the things I can, and the wisdom to know the difference." This well-known quote from theologian Reinhold Niebuhr has many applications in life, but I think it can be central to Masters on their journey. Unfortunately, many of us will be blind to this teaching until it clobbers us over the head. Rare is the Master who will find himself with a slave who is a perfect match, or who will be the perfect clay from which to form his vision of the ultimate slave. I have found that my path to Mastery has included many decisions about how to approach and handle the situations where the reality of my slave conflicts with the perfection of my vision. I feel that within these decisions I have found some of the more meaningful milestones in my journey.

A note on definitions: For purposes of this writing I will use the words Master and slave, as these are the terms I apply to my own dynamic. Similarly, I refer to genders as they exist in my dynamic. While reading this, please feel free to substitute your own genders and preferred terminology for M-type and s-type roles, as I feel what I am writing can apply to any power exchange dynamic.

To better understand the context for what I am about to explore, it would help to understand a bit more about who I am, and how I got to where I am now in my journey into Mastery. I am a Master who entered into power exchange from a pre-existing relationship. My slave and I have successfully transitioned a marriage, which has now spanned nearly thirty years, into a thriving Master/slave power exchange. This transition took place over many years, but started in earnest about seventeen years into our marriage. The seeds of our power exchange go back much further to the very beginning, but they had to be nurtured and understood to reach their full potential. We arrived at the start of our journey into M/s with many years of partnership under our belts, and although many things needed to change, others I found could not, or should not be transformed.

Some Masters will have the luxury to try out many slaves, looking for that one they believe best fits their vision. Others of us are destined to work with the person we have, and that fact is reflected in the challenge embodied in the quote above. I was firmly in that second category, as the partner with whom I started my M/s journey was already my cherished life partner. I had a slave full of potential, eager to serve me and ready to be led and even changed in many ways, but as a new Master, with my head filled with the visions of what a Master "should be", I was blind to the Master I needed to be, at least for a while.

Many who are new to power exchange on the M side think that Mastery is all about getting our needs met in the exact way we want by our slave. I initially believed that I must exert total authority in decision-making, forming the complete vision of what our dynamic must look like and exactly how my slave must change to fit that vision. The clay would have to yield so that I could do my job fulfilling the leadership role intended in our mutually-agreed power exchange. It was an intoxicating thought, and there is actually a basic truth there about the role of the Master—to lead with vision and create the structure for the relationship is central to the job. It is a sentiment I hear from the various corners of our community to this day, but it is often expressed in black and white terms that emphasize the all-powerful all-visionary nature of the Master and the all-adaptable all-supporting nature of the slave. More seldom do I hear shades of grey talked about in helpful meaningful ways. It's probably not that the people talking don't understand or believe in that balance, but rather that power exchange is most easily talked about from the "ideals". It is easy to discuss ideals and more difficult to discuss actualities, as these will tend to be very specific to the dynamic and individuals involved, with nuance and texture not easily described to others.

For the beginning Master, not yet secure or experienced in finding a balance, there exists a hazard in talking about idealized power exchange. It can result in them striving for an unattainable ideal at the expense of what might be a fulfilling actuality. For example, without the grounding of experience in my early days of Mastery, I found myself unsure and reluctant to accept much input from my slave at all regarding certain aspects which I thought ventured into my realm of visionary authority. I thought that if the genesis of an idea was not strictly from me, it was therefore somehow suspect and not in support of my own path towards Mastery. I was uncomfortable when my slave would bring suggestions for protocols and rituals, as the ideas did not originate with me. I later came to understand that things such as protocols and rituals, regardless of who conceived of them, only have value if they serve my needs and wants or the needs of the dynamic (which includes my slave's needs). I was too insecure that my Mastery would be undermined to accept that reasonable input from my slave. I made the beginner mistake of not recognizing my slave as a resource—*my* resource. With time and experience, I have found that it is not important where or from whom an idea comes; if it suits me and my dynamic, adopting it is a testament to my Mastery, not a challenge to it.

While protocols and rituals can be important, as they lay significant foundations on which to build, strengthen and experience an M/s dynamic, the real important work of Mastery comes in deciding what more fundamental behaviors or traits can or should be changed with regard to one's slave or one's self. Note that I strongly believe that Mastery is as much about the evolution of the Master as it is of the slave. Most Masters never fully and truly envision these implications when they start their journey. This is where the hard work begins. Striking the correct balance on such deeper internal changes for one's slave and one's self sorts the would-be Masters from the more successful and enlightened Masters.

It remains a common misconception that a Master can simply decide to change their slave in fundamental ways. While this may be possible, I contend that fundamental change is the exception and not the rule. Often the attitude towards changing the slave is expressed as if it were as simple as the Master setting forth a vision and the slave working to realize it. (Consideration is seldom expressed regarding whether the slave has a fundamental inability or conflicting need that gets in the way of the Master's vision.) I want to pause here and say that for some dynamics this may work. I would follow by saying that in my experience, such dynamics are not typical. The reason for this is that I have yet to meet a slave that is either a such a perfect match or so perfectly adaptable to their Master's needs and wants that their needs do not need to be considered in the Master's decision making.

A concrete example from my own experience, where the perfection of my vision ran into an unexpected reality with regards to my slave, centered around monogamy. During the process of transforming our egalitarian marriage into an M/s power exchange dynamic, the idea occurred to me to consider changing the nature of our relationship from strict monogamy to something more open. I consider myself polyamory-curious, and wanted to pursue these interests. In my excitement as a new Master I failed to realize that my slave is strongly monogamous. It is not just a "want" for her, but rather a fundamental need rooted deep in her psyche and nature, and that is an important distinction. In my eagerness to mold my slave to fit my poly curiosity, I failed to understand the importance of working with the slave before me rather than molding an ideal. Referring back to the quote I mentioned above, I ran into something I had to "accept", not something I could "change". What I lacked initially was the wisdom to know the difference.

Let me clarify this example further. For me, poly-curiosity is a want rather than a need, but in looking only to my own counsel on setting a vision to explore this concept, I was making a mistake in my personal Mastery. I thought that as Master it was my purview alone to decide what was a reasonable path for our dynamic to explore. I chose to open a series of discussions regarding monogamy. Let me be clear: I was not dictating a choice for us to go out and start pursuing non-monogamous encounters. I wanted to begin discussions and entertain the ideas. Now this decision on its face may seem completely reasonable, and for some dynamics it would be a perfectly benign conversation. Through repeated negative outcomes, however, I realized that for us there was more behind this topic than a simple hypothetical discussion. But rather than fully understand the need to delve deeper into the underlying conflict, I continued having the same discussions assuming I would eventually be able to mold my slave to my way of thinking.

What I thought I had presented as a *hypothetical* possibility of a poly future in our discussions was perceived as a direct conflict with a fundamental need. My slave balked, unable to see these discussions as hypothetical. When we dug in a little further we found that I had made a critical mistake. I did not work to get to the bottom of the issue and understand what was behind my slave's perception, so I was not able to consider her needs in my decision making to have these conversations. While this issue seems straightforward when seen as polyamory in conflict with monogamy, my slave was not most upset or distraught over my poly desires, but rather over her fear that she would not be able to follow where I was leading. The need I was violating was the one in which she desperately needed to follow me, but was afraid she would not be able to do so if she could not meet my vision for the future of our relationship. This had invoked an intense fear response. She knew herself well enough to know that she was herself not capable of pursuing anything in the poly realm, though she fully respected and understood poly concepts and relationships for others, including me.

So as I continued to bring up the subject to try to have what I thought were "safe" exploratory discussions, I was encountering intense negative reactions that, to me, seemed out of proportion to the situation at hand. This frustrated me. At one point, after a particularly spectacular end to a disaster of a conversation (a.k.a. a big emotional argument), I finally understand that discussing poly concepts in the context of our personal dynamic was not going to work, but I also felt that it had escalated into a challenge to my authority in the dynamic. I felt this was a violation of my own needs, and there was a great disconnect here. My slave was having a fear reaction which I did not yet fully understand, and I was feeling challenged in my authority, which my slave didn't understand.

While this was really a communication issue—which was ultimately resolved—it is an example of the complicated interactions and intense emotions that occur when navigating the areas of a dynamic that touch upon challenging subjects, including and especially things that cannot or should not be changed.

Invariably, as Masters we will all face situations where our decisions can really matter to the dynamic. Sometimes these are not all or nothing moments, but rather something that plays out over longer periods of time—many small decisions, many interactions. The recurring series of encounters I have described fits this latter model. Over time I had run into a situation that needed more attention and more decisiveness, tenacity and leadership than I had probably initially considered it might require. Seemingly small things can turn into existential crises. In this case there were several areas that needed to be addressed. The easiest was the original question of poly exploration. It was a relatively simple decision, once I finally knew all the facts about my slave's monogamous fabric, to set aside my curiosity and focus instead on developing the rich M/s relationship we were forging together. This was not something I needed to try to change in my slave, and there was far richer soil to till in the garden of our dynamic.

However, the fear reaction I had stoked in my slave was somewhat harder to deal with. Fear is a powerful reaction and it can cause many different undesirable effects, one of which is that it becomes a block for the slave to commit to deeper surrender. Building the trust that she could indeed follow me, that we were on a path that would take us forward together, became the reassurance needed in this case to combat the fear-induced effects. Such experiences are not all together negative, though, since it is through navigating such trials and challenges and persevering, that deeper M/s is often achieved.

Finally, the hardest of all to deal were my own inner conflicts. Some were specific to the situation at hand, some were around my overarching path towards Mastery. Despite ultimately leading us through this difficult (for us) topic and process—which I know helped grow my Mastery, and which I consider a success—I spent a lot of time looking back on the entire episode, critiquing and analyzing my handling of the various elements. It is my belief that many self-aware Masters are harder on themselves than their slaves are on them. I faced many questions about myself: Did I lead as well as I could have? What were the challenges to my leadership, both internal and external? Did I make the right decisions at the right times? What could I have done better? This self-questioning is the hardest part in many ways, since as a Master I am never done asking and re-asking these types of questions. The path of Mastery can be very lonely, as we keep our own counsel so often.

In the end, as the quote indicates, I gained the wisdom to understand I had discovered within my slave something I should not change, and I achieved the serenity to accept it. This wisdom and serenity allowed me to realize a greater appreciation for the great gift that is my slave, and the ability to fully see to the depths of her slaveheart. I learned a great deal about her devotion to me and our dynamic through this troubling set of interactions. While it was difficult to navigate at the time, the journey afforded me many insights, including a fuller understanding of the distinction between needs, wants and desires both for myself and for my slave, and how I must balance and prioritize them within the context of our dynamic. As I continue to grow in my Mastery, it remains my firm belief that my decisions not only shape my vision for our dynamic, but also serve the greater good of that dynamic. As we navigate this journey into M/s, I have had the courage to change the things I *could* change for the betterment of both my slave and myself, but I remain guided in the principle that I must always exercise wisdom in so doing.

*Master Jim is the Director of MAsT Massachusetts. He and his slave dee married out of college and have been exploring kink ever since. They entered the Leather lifestyle in 2010 and successfully transitioned their happy marriage into a thriving M/s dynamic. An MTTA alum, Master Jim enjoys teaching and giving back to the Leather and BDSM communities. In his spare time he can be found playing pinball and making espresso.*

# Bouncing Off Boundaries

*Jason Dietrich*

We all like to fantasize about being in a Master/slave relationship where the Master controls every little thing about the slave. Well, all right, some of us do! But it's not always possible in every situation, and that's something we have to accept. The truth is that the vast majority of D/s and M/s relationships are not situations where the dominant partner has authority over everything. In most cases, there are areas where it isn't appropriate or possible for the Master to be given authority. Some of these might include:

❖ Children, especially if they are not the Master's children, but come in from a former relationship. The slave may feel that the children did not consent to be under the Master's authority, and therefore the slave will protect them from that possibility.

❖ Co-parents of said children, which includes issues of custody, child support, visitation, and other decisions that the other parent did not agree to share with their ex-partner's new squeeze.

❖ Existing partners. If the slave is polyamorous, they may come in with pre-existing lovers who did not consent to have their situation disrupted by the demands of a new relationship. In most cases, this will require a lot of communication by all parties to make sure that pre-existing relationships will feel respected.

❖ Family. They likely have seniority in the slave's life, and unless the relationship is so toxic that the Master wants to separate them for their own safety—a decision which perhaps should be made with the help of a therapist—they will likely not appreciate those relationships being interfered with.

❖ Careers, especially ones where the slave has confidentiality with clients, patients, the government, etc. If the slave's career—and all decisions regarding it—require very specialized knowledge that the Master doesn't have, then it could be disastrous for them to insert themselves into the equation.

❖ Finances, especially if there are major debts, property that is jointly held with someone else, businesses co-owned with someone else, or the aforementioned stepchildren to support.

❖ Major health issues. If the slave has been handling something like this for their whole life, they know a lot more about it than their new Master, and it may be important to them to keep control of all decisions surrounding their health practices.

❖ Gender expression. If the slave has a nonstandard gender identity, they have probably spent their lives fighting for the right to express that identity, and the Master needs to respect that or they won't keep that slave long.

❖ Similarly, belonging to any minority group—perhaps around race, sexual orientation, ethnicity, etc.—can include emotionally important activities with other people in that group, which the Master should probably keep their hands off unless they are also part of that group.

❖ Political work, if it is important to the slave, and voting.

❖ Religion, if it is important to the slave. This is especially important if the Master is nonreligious, or dislikes religion, or belongs to a faith that is traditionally antagonistic to the slave's faith.

There are certainly relationships where the slave puts any or all of these things under the Master's authority. However, this is usually when the slave fully trusts that they are both absolutely on the same page anyway, and it wouldn't create a problem. It's rarest for the situations involving other people; generally the other people need to really like and respect the Master and believe that the Master's good judgment is extremely beneficial for the slave's life, and for their own when it affects their decisions through the slave's decisions. This can happen without those individuals ever knowing about the M/s relationship; the slave can just make it clear that they admire and trust this person so much, and that their track record has turned out to be so good, that it makes sense for the slave to ask their advice all the time.

Sometimes the slave might put one or more of these areas under the authority of a Master because they are having a hard time managing them, and damage has occurred because of that poor handling. What the slave needs to know is that all of these issues (as well as any major ones I may have missed here) are heavy weights on a Master. Asking them to take charge of these areas, especially if the Master will be inheriting a big mess to clean up, is a great deal of work and responsibility. Saying "Here, Master, handle my thousands of dollars of student debt, my serious illness about which you know nothing, and my five children whose other parent doesn't like you!" is not a favor to them.

What the Master needs to realize is that they are also allowed to set boundaries and say no to something. There is no shame in saying, "That's beyond my time, energy, and skills to take on right now. Perhaps I might take it on some day in the future, but right now you need to keep taking care of it." Some Masters will be fine with taking responsibility even for big messes, eventually if not in the beginning, but no Master should agree to take responsibility for any area where they are not confident of their ability to smoothly handle things. Don't get carried away by a feeling of wanting to impress your slave with how competent you are. Serious life areas like this are not an appropriate place to take risks, and if you make errors, you will let your slave down and possibly make a bad situation worse. It's also possible that you may be grateful not to have to deal with certain areas of your slave's life.

Here's where I make it personal. The person in my service now is not the person I started this journey with, or the second one either. I made a lot of mistakes along the way, and I'd like to believe that I didn't make the same mistake twice. With my first submissive, I thought that M/s naturally ought to lead to me taking control of everything, and I felt like a failure for not being able to convince my submissive that this was the right idea. Instead of seeing my submissive's boundaries as something I needed to respect in order to maintain trust, I resented them. That resentment found its way into the relationship, and contributed to our breakup.

My second submissive (who ultimately became my slave) did eventually allow me to take over a lot more areas of life than the last one, and some of them (like my slave's mental health problems) I found myself completely unprepared for. Frankly, I made a mess of it. I meant well and I tried hard, but I ended up thrashing around trying random solutions in the hope that something would work, and I just made it worse. It would have been better if I'd just allowed those boundaries to stay where they were, at least until I had a lot more experience and understanding. That relationship, too, fell by the wayside. In a way it was even worse, because I'd raised hopes in my slave that ended up being dashed.

I came to my third submissive a much-chastened master. I'd learned that respecting boundaries wasn't merely an insult to my authority; it might well be a blessing while I figured out what I could reasonably take on. My willingness to respect those boundaries from the beginning created more trust, and my hard-earned lessons in compromise continue that trust today. There are still areas where my now-slave retains authority. Will that ever change? Maybe, maybe not, but I don't dwell on it, Instead, I focus on what I do have, and in stewarding and managing that to the best of my ability. My slave focuses on not letting those areas interfere too much in our power exchange. We've learned to trust each other in this dance.

So what happens when you must navigate the edges between the areas of life where you have control, and the ones where you don't? Will it ever clash? Of course it will. That's just life, and you will have to be mature and reasonable about the situation. My first suggestion to you is to sit down with your slave and list all the areas of their life, and discuss the degree of influence you are allowed to have in each one. It helped me to draw them all out visually like the countries in a continent, with similar areas next to each other, and then color them with different colors. Getting a visual helped me to picture it in my mind.

The Degrees of Influence are:

❖ *No influence at all.* In this area, the slave isn't even required to tell the Master about it, unless something from that area is going to impinge on the Master's everyday life and/or the workings of the power dynamic. *Example: The slave had a private conversation with their other partner which left them somewhat emotional. They tell their Master that the conversation happened, and that it will have an effect on their mood tonight, but it is not appropriate to reveal the details of the conversation because they've promised their other partner privacy.*

❖ **Informational Influence.** The slave is required to tell the Master everything about the situation, ideally in a timely manner, so that the Master can make plans accordingly, working around the obstacles of the external circumstances. The Master, however, has no actual say over the activities. *Example: The Master wants to have an intimate weekend away with some kinky sex, but the slave gets called in to work for a career emergency on the scheduled weekend, or the slave's child from their former marriage gets sick and it's their turn to take the kid to the doctor. Luckily the slave told the Master the second it happened, so the reservation for that nice beach house could be rescheduled.*

❖ **Advisory Influence.** The Master is allowed to advise the slave about the area, whether or not the slave asks for advice. The slave is not obligated to follow the advice, but some couples agree that the slave will at least take the Master's advice very seriously, and only reject it if they feel that there is an extremely good reason. One slave who uses this system said, "Me being inconvenienced, annoyed, or scared of something it would be better if I faced down is not a sufficient reason." Of course, every Master/slave couple will need to negotiate under what circumstances the slave can ignore the Master's advice. It's also important for the Master to seriously consider how they will feel when that happens. If the slave is simply exercising a negotiated right to put that advice aside, even if the Master feels that the slave is really on the wrong track, how will the Master force themselves to honorably stand aside and let the slave have the consequences of their own decision? It might be useful for the Master to work on internal tools to use in that moment, such as journaling about it, talking to a friend or therapist, going for a long walk, or distracting themselves with some other engrossing activity. *Example: The Master advises that the slave should quit their rather stressful job and find a different one. The slave wants to hang on for one more year in order to get better severance pay benefits,* *and feels that it will be worth it, but it is a hard choice that only they can decide.*

❖ ***Total Influence.*** At this degree, the Master has been given full authority to make decisions in this area of the slave's life.

Just because a compromise is negotiated, however, does not mean that it will always be easy, both practically and emotionally. The slave may feel guilty that they cannot give over this activity. The Master may feel resentful—perhaps not so much that they can't have that one thing per se, but more likely because they are dreaming of a total power exchange and that's not possible due to life circumstances. They may also be upset when—as we've mentioned above—the non-controlled areas of the slave's life get in the way of the controlled areas. *Example: The Master supposedly has been given authority over the slave's appearance, and would like the slave to alter that appearance in some way—perhaps a not-easily-hidden tattoo or a large visible locked-on collar—but that would create a problem with their job, which is not under the Master's authority. The Master may feel that their control over the slave's appearance is not real or meaningful because they keep being thwarted by other concerns.*

It is sometimes hard for Masters when they have conflicting feelings about the situation. However, in the rest of life, dealing maturely with ambiguous situations over which one has little control is just part of being a functional adult. (After all, who among us really enjoys standing in line at the Registry of Motor Vehicles?) If the relationship is committed and the couple intends to be together for the rest of their lives, then sometimes plans can be put in place to eventually hand that area over to the Master at a future date, perhaps when a particular goal has been achieved. Children grow up, careers eventually move into retirement, and Masters can dedicate themselves to learning all about certain parts of the slave's life, thus earning the right to make decisions there. On the other hand, some situations are just going to remain out of reach permanently, and the Master has to master themselves and their emotions, and never sabotage the slave in that area. Being a Master is a great responsibility, and we need to be honorable people. To subtly discourage or interfere with an area of the slave's life which is out of your control because you resent its existence is not an honorable act.

One thing to keep in mind when it comes to the Degrees of Influence as I listed them above is that over many years the lines can become more blurry. A slave who makes a habit of asking advice in an area may eventually just get to the point where they just take the Master's advice all the time out of habit, and unconsciously "forget" that they have the right to reject it. It's also possible that the slave may start making decisions in a particular non-controlled area based on how they suit the Master rather than what is best for the slave, or the others involved. This may be due to infatuation, fear of disapproval or abandonment, or subtle pressure from the Master's annoyance. An ethical Master who notices this happening will call the slave's attention to it, and request that the slave make decisions based on healthier reasons that take everyone into account. They should insist on this even if it makes their own life less easy, because we as Masters need to be looking at the future rather than simply trying to arrange our own convenience. Showing that you care about the slave's well-being more than your own short-term desires builds trust in your judgment.

Speaking of trust: The Master also has to trust the slave to make good decisions in the non-controlled areas of their life—decisions that, while they may not cater to the Master's whims, do take the relationship and its future into account. *Example: The slave has the chance at a higher-paying job, but it will require many more hours and there will be less time for service to the Master, and a focus on the relationship. After discussing and deliberating, the slave decides to find a job with lower pay but more flexible hours.*

This only works if the Master is very clear about the Vision they have for the relationship, and the slave thoroughly understands and agrees with that vision. It may help for the Master to check on the slave's clear understanding by asking periodic questions—"What do you think, in a situation like X, would be the best choice to move toward our future goals?" If the slave is unclear about where the Master wants to go—or if the Master has no clear mission in mind themselves—it sets the slave up to make decisions that may turn out to be obstacles in the end.

Bouncing around between these boundaries can be a very delicate game, but it's a crucial one, because it makes consent real. This is not to say that slaves in total power exchange relationships didn't consent freely and willingly to giving over their whole lives— one hopes that they did!—but as M/s people, we hold consent to be sacred. What this means is that a slave's "Yes" means as much as their "No". If they can't set a boundary and have it respected—not just grudgingly but with a real appreciation for how this is an important part of this vital person—then this casts doubts on the freely given nature of their assent to pass over control. As the people who receive huge and extreme gifts of devotion and privilege from our slaves, we need to show them—and the world, to some extent—that we are mature, honorable people who can walk up to a negotiated boundary and go no further, not even to poke it with a toe. It's all part of building deep trust, without which this dance could never go on.

———◗●◖———

*Jason Dietrich is a Master living in the Midwest with a wonderful slave-wife, five dogs, two cats, and a horse. He is active in his local MAsT (Masters And slaves Together) group and cracks a mean bullwhip.*

# Compromising With Reality
*Raven Kaldera*

I like to say that I don't compromise with my slaveboy. I compromise with reality.

*Reality is* that we are part of a large polyamorous family, most of whom live together in one old farmhouse, with differing levels of power exchange between us, ranging from completely egalitarian to completely owned. We've also had various friends living with us who weren't involved with any of us sexually or romantically. We don't live the fantasy model that everyone thinks of when they consider M/s— one master living only with people whom they own, in a kinky and isolated little world of their own where people are kept naked and chained and spankings might happen over the breakfast table. Some of our members might be OK with that, but some didn't consent to seeing that over breakfast in the public areas of the house, and aren't likely to do so. This means that unless we're alone together in a room, my slaveboy and I need to be considerate and discreet. "Honey, could you get me a drink?" becomes code for "Get me a drink, boy." "Is there still fish left over from last night?" becomes code for "Feed me, bitch." (Reality also includes the fact that the old farmhouse is poorly heated and we live in New England, so no one dares to be naked in the public areas of the house for at least half the year.)

*Reality is* that I hold a leadership role in our church, which often holds its potlucks in our old farmhouse as well as meaning various church members might be coming and going a great deal of the time. Discretion holds there, too—some church members are theoretically aware of our power dynamic, and some aren't, but none of them are comfortable with seeing one of their church leaders treat his partner in a way that could be construed as abusive. Knowing intellectually that our relationship is entirely consensual, that Joshua loves being my boy, doesn't help in the face of the strong emotions that the trappings of a power dynamic bring up for some people—especially people with abuse histories. It's Joshua's job to simply appear to be my happy and helpful boyfriend who just happens to always want to do whatever I want to do, and it's my job to appear kind and generous and affectionate, just like a good vanilla partner. I also present on non-M/s topics at other venues, and he comes along as my helpful personal assistant, but even there I know we're scrutinized and must appear non-threatening.

On the other hand, this reality means that Joshua spends the "public" parts of our life hiding our actual reality, and this wears on him. He's not my boyfriend. He's my property. Some couples might have no trouble integrating both of those roles, but that doesn't work for us. Those words, those roles have too much of an egalitarian feel to them, and there is no part of our relationship that is egalitarian. There is certainly reciprocity, in that we both have to give a certain amount of energy and effort to the relationship or it won't work, but there is nothing that I don't have the right to attempt to change if I wanted to risk it … and he has no recourse if I decide to do so. That's what he agreed to, more than a decade and a half ago. That's the deal, and we both like it that way. So it's my job to make sure that he has time and space with me where it's openly acknowledged that he's my property and not my boyfriend, and we act accordingly. Otherwise the dissonance is crazy-making for him, and I don't want that.

*Reality is* that everyone in our household is disabled in some way. Of the six members of our poly family who live here part or all of the time, half are actually on disability payments for various ailments ranging from fibromyalgia to brain damage, another will be going there soon, and I'd certainly be there as well if my book royalty payments didn't make me just barely too much to qualify (although not enough for a decent living wage). Our house motto is "We are patient with one another", because we have to be. The public walkways of the house need to be free of breakables lower than shoulder height, because the person with brain damage from a car accident might have a dizzy spell and fall into them. The "arms" we installed on the toilet so that the arthritic person can get up mean that the person with pituitary gigantism can't use it, so another toilet must be put in. We've put in a stair chair; we're putting in a wheelchair ramp to the house and an accessible bathroom. When house meetings contain one person with fibro fog and ADD, another with lupus fog and chronic pain, another with brain damage, another with Asperger's Syndrome, and three who are on psych meds, we learn to write *everything* down, and we learn to live by lists and more lists and shared Google calendars.

This means that some days it's a matter of "There's a difficult job to be done. Who's least impaired today?" If my slaveboy isn't on that list at the moment, he'll feel awful, especially if it means that I end up doing it. His service is very important to his sense of identity, and while usually he is my PCA and takes care of my physical issues, there are days when he's down and the positions are reversed. (Occasionally we are both down at the same time and can only lie in bed together and moan, but at least there's a sense of mute visceral caring and support for each other.)

Service has also been important to boys I've had in the past, one of whom came to me with crippling fibromyalgia and a host of neurological problems, afraid that no one would ever want him to serve because his illnesses were such a stumbling block. This, however, was just a matter of creativity, and of finding ways to serve at every level of shifting ability. A boy who couldn't get out of bed on a particular day could still do Internet research for me on a light laptop or tablet, or sort my voluminous medications, or knit me something, or find me addresses and phone numbers in my email when I call home from another state saying, "We're at the place where I'm supposed to teach and no one is here!" When he was so bad off that he could only be a lump in bed, he could still be a backrest or a lap desk or a footwarmer. (Since I have Reynaud's syndrome, which gives me frighteningly cold hands and feet in cold weather, there was a certain amount of gleeful sadism in the application of the latter job. Fortunately he was a masochist, and we worked in our jollies wherever we can.) Sometimes we could only manage what we referred to as "crip sex", which is an exchange of massage for our aching bodies … and sometimes that was almost better than sex itself. On days when he couldn't even manage that, then his service to me was to rest and do what was necessary to get past this particular flare.

*Reality is* that my slaveboy's Asperger's Syndrome means that there are tasks he can't manage very well, and it's my job to take this into account and not repeatedly set him up for failure. If he comes to me in the middle of the party where he's serving and says, "Sir, I really need to go be in a quiet place for a while," I know that he's at the end of his neurological rope. I trust him not to "tap out" unless he is absolutely sure that he can't go any further without a meltdown, and I'll immediately order some destimulation time for him. I have no patience with masters who act like their s-type's known limitations are some kind of affront to their authority. For that matter, if you have an s-type with a disability, there's no excuse for not learning everything you can about it. It's like refusing to look at the owner's manual while complaining that you can't get the thing to work. Real power over someone requires knowledge and study of them and their inner workings, especially the monkey wrenches in their system.

*Reality is* that while we are all massively kinky, illness often gets in the way of sex. Sometimes I'm in too much pain to do anything except recline against pillows and perhaps limply beat off a bit ... and how do you keep your feeling of confidence as a master when you can barely move? By giving commands, of course. "Fuck yourself for me. Entertain me. Turn around so I can see that better. Get me something light to hit you with, something that will hurt like hell with the least possible effort for me. Get your ass over here to where I can fuck it." The boys call it being a "helpful victim", as opposed to a helpless one. It reminds them that I don't need a body to assert my authority, that it isn't based on superiority of body but superiority of will. I learned well the lesson of Thulsa Doom, the villain in that first corny *Conan The Barbarian* movie, who waved a hand and a slave willingly jumped to her death while he said, "You see, boy? Flesh is stronger than steel."

The flip side of this reality is that sometimes my partners aren't up for sex either, even the ones who have sworn never to refuse sex with me. It's my job to decide whether it's worth it to push them—do I want to have sex with someone who's miserable? Some sadists might be into that, but I much prefer enthusiasm, and I'm willing to compromise with reality and wait until they can give me that. They are not controlling me or even setting limits when they say, "Sir, I'm feeling really awful, this part of me hurts, I don't think I can muster any enthusiasm for sex right now." They are not saying No, they are giving me useful information which with to make a measured decision. They know I could override them and force it anyway, but I generally don't do that. It makes more sense to keep sex an entirely positive thing for both of us, and all mastery is risk assessment anyway. One of the marks of a good master, to me, is being able to maturely accept the compromise with reality and not allow resentment to seep into your decisions.

*Reality is* that because of these limitations, we do share a low-income life together. Sometimes we struggle to keep the household's various heads above water, and someone's old car dying is a major emergency, because there may not be money to replace it. Unlike the pornography where masters are all rich and slaves are kept in kinky luxury, we can rarely afford kink conferences or fancy anything. My slaveboy learned how to fix plumbing out of sheer self-defense, and I'm grateful for that. Having accessible bathrooms is less glamorous but much more useful than having newer cars or fancy electronics, or for that matter pretty collars. A dog chain will do and can be found at the dollar store. I don't need that leather clothing, I need a respirator to protect my highly-allergic lungs from smoke and petroleum fumes when we go out. (One of my partners has already eroticized the respirator and the leg braces, and calls me his "dearest Sith Lord".) We know what's important and we focus on that.

Far too much power exchange literature posits these relationships as happening in affluent circumstances. Slaves don't have to work jobs, because the master can afford to keep them like pets or housewives. While some people in this lifestyle are living like that, far more that I know of are struggling financially and the fantasy must be sacrificed to the reality of survival. This doesn't mean that M/s ends when the slave walks out the door to go to work. On the contrary, I think of my slaveboy's jobs as me "renting" him out, even if those to whom I rent his hands don't know that's going on. I'd like to see more written examples of low-income M/s—one can be devoted and obedient in a tiny, cheap apartment. In a lot of ways, there's more honor in both parties holding to their agreement under difficult circumstances than when things are easy and stress-free.

*Reality is* that we've found troubleshooting to be far more effective than punishment. An incidence of apparent disobedience is picked over and analyzed to find out where it went wrong, and solutions are brainstormed and experimented with in order to prevent it happening again. I'd much rather solve the problem than vent my anger and frustration. I want a smoothly running system more than I want a place where it's OK to tantrum at a partner like a two-year-old. Some people have asked me, "Do you use fear as a tool when disciplining your s-types?" Considering that for the past twenty years I've only ended up with boys who have anxiety disorders—"disorder" in the sense that they have been medicated for it at least once in their lives—fear is a counterproductive tool. Instead, I do a lot of calming them down—"OK, now breathe. Breathe deep. Put your head between my feet. Everything is going to be OK. We're going to figure this out."

It's important to me that my slaveboy obeys because it's important to him to feel like he's doing a good job, not because he fears consequences. To me, feeling empowered when one gets it right is a healthier motivation than fear of getting it wrong. Some s-types do require a punishment context for whatever reason, and there are plenty of M-types who prefer that as well for them to pick from, but to me, repeated deliberate disobedience is more likely to make me ask "So, do you really want to be here? Because you're not acting like you do." However, in nearly every case for us, apparent "disobedience" is actually an external monkey wrench that has fallen into the system—fatigue, distraction, memory issues, misunderstanding orders, overwhelming stress, miscalculation of resources, etc.—and it's much simpler and easier on everyone to just locate and remove the wrench, and try again with routines in place to prevent it falling back in.

That's really what our protocols are for—well, the ones that aren't designed around my disabilities, to help my slaveboy manage my body and its awkwardnesses. He says "Yes, Sir" to anything he thinks is an order, not because it makes me feel powerful or even that it reifies our power dynamic or shows respect. I came up with that protocol because it lets me know that he heard me (trickier than you'd think in a busy household), he understands that this is an order and not a random comment … and if it's not actually an order, I can correct that. While it does show respect and willingness to obey, it is primarily a communication tool to prevent misunderstandings. With all the neurological differences in this house, protocols are more for prevention of problems than for making anyone feel good.

*Reality is* that we don't always feel one hundred per cent confident about our power dynamic "jobs", and that includes me. Just as the boys might occasionally go into a spasm of self-loathing over the imperfect nature of their service, I sometimes spend nights lying awake worrying that I'm not skilled enough to make this work smoothly. Days where my pain levels require me to take a break from decision-making can put me into a tailspin of worry about my competence at the job. Days when I make an error because I misjudged how much my physical state was affecting my mental state are particularly difficult. It's hard not to feel ashamed of one's own limitations when they impinge on one's decision-making capacity, when decision-making is one's full-time job. I've got PTSD on top of all the physical issues, and sometimes that also rears up and catches me, and I make less than stellar decisions. This has frightened my boys a great deal in the beginning, and I had to suck it up, breathe, and have discussions about my PTSD patterns. I enlisted them to help me to be mindful, rather than pretending that it wasn't happening. (OK, I did do some of that when we started, but I eventually came to terms with the fact that it had to be dealt with, because it was affecting my functioning.) I can feel better about being an imperfect human being by reminding myself that I'm on a Team with some competent subordinates who are more interested in solving problems than being judgmental or maintaining their fantasies.

I'm lucky in that I have s-types who see an admission of a problem as strength and honesty rather than evidence of non-domliness, who see a request for help as an opportunity for service rather than as a weakness, and who admire someone who finds compensatory mechanisms for their problems instead of lapsing into despair. My slaveboy is understanding about my scars, and he admires the strength it took to get past them, and I try hard to respect his. This is something the ubiquitous porn-model ignores, or even denigrates—M-types are supposed to be perfect, or at least tough rocks who never break or make errors. On the other side, s-types are supposed to be perfect as well, never having days when they just want to throw it all up in the air and scream.

However, my power dynamic relationships live in Reality, and the upshot of this is that they make Reality a whole lot more functional. When I need to be able to get down a flight of stairs on a shaky day with some manner of dignity, I have a boy to become my railing. When I need him to refrain from eating food in front of me that I want but can't have because of my medical issues, he will happily acquiesce. If reality is sharp edges, power dynamics can provide some padding all around. Make it work with your reality rather than trying to manifest a fantasy. The results are a lot more sustainable—my slaveboy and I have been together for seventeen years now—and will gently move with you in the reality of where every life eventually, inevitably goes.

# Intentional Thought:
# A Short Essay About Rules and Protocols
*PackMaster Doug*

Protocols and rituals are a misunderstood tenet of M/s relationships. A protocol can range from something simple as asking permission to leave the Master's presence to something more complex like a prescribed way to present Master with a drink or enter Master's bed. These "practiced manners" have a calculated undertone. Protocols put a "thought step" into natural actions, and the thought persists until something/someone else replaces it.

As an example: I was at the wedding of a former slave. A group of us were standing around talking, including the bride-to-be. Suddenly, she leaned into me and whispered, "Master, may I go to the bathroom?" Granted, on some level this was meant as humorous, but there still was the idea/thought that leaving my side required my permission. Widowed slaves have reported to me that years after the loss of their Masters, they still looked around expecting their Master to give permission for a simple task the vanilla world would take for granted, like leaving a space or going to the bathroom.

The thoughts I'd like to leave all the newer Masters are: First, you can use protocols to shape "thought reminders" for your slaves. Protocols and rules provide the slave with a strong sense of connection and bonding. The "extra thought level" needed to execute these protocols becomes an intentional thought of and about the relationship with the one who has designed that protocol.

For example: If, when away from you at work, your slave has to go to the restroom and you have a rule that they must ask permission when they are with you, even when you're not there the first instinct will be to check for that permission. You've added a moment of your slave being connected to you, of them not being alone.

Secondly, a Master must be thoughtful and judicious in the rituals and protocols they instill in their relationship. Keep in mind that your "re-education" and protocols might not just end when you leave the slave. The slave will carrying your training with them forever, or until it wears off, or until someone else has the time and energy to undo it. If you release a slave, it is worth it to do some preliminary work to help them shake off those habits.

———————○———————

*PackMaster Doug lives in Phoenix, AZ. He is a retired educator who has been doing M/s for 40+ years, and is the Director of MAsT Greater Phoenix Chapter, the former facilitator for the Arizona Power Exchange (APEX) Dominant Roundtable, and the former facilitator APEX Polyamory Special Interest Group. He lives in a Poly M/s/s household with two live-in slaves.*

# Advice for the Single Master

John "Bannor" Orr

> *Michi wo hiraku Tamashii no VISION Stand Proud!*
> *(Paving one's own road with the vision of one's spirt, Stand Proud!)*
>
> – Jin Hashimoto, Stand Proud.

Welcome! If you are reading this than the chances are that you have entered the M/s lifestyle as a single unattached Master. I am glad to have you here in this community. As of this writing, I have been single for over four years while looking for a slave, and I have learned a few survival tips and tricks along my path that I would like to share with you. If you are not a single Master and just reading this out of curiosity, feel free to continue but understand that this essay isn't aimed at you and there might be concepts that you don't agree with or understand.

For those who are concerned about titles, I am using "Master" to denote someone, regardless of gender, who is interested being in a 24/7 total power exchange as the authority figure in that relationship. "Slave" is used to denote someone who in giving up their authority in that 24/7 total power exchange relationship. If these titles do not fit your definition, feel free to change them as you see fit.

Let us first recognize that being a single Master in this lifestyle is incredibly difficult. You will see a lot of people engaging in activities and displays of affection that you long to experience (or used to experience). It may feel like these types of relationships come easily to everyone in this community except you. When you are in space that is predominantly for couples, being single can feel excruciatingly lonely. It is not uncommon to feel that the reason you are alone is because there is something wrong with you.

You may also find that as welcoming as the M/s community claims to be, you still might feel not welcome in that space. I know what it is like to go to regional Kink/Leather conferences and feel left out, when everyone is with their MAsT chapter and partners and I am by myself. I count conferences where I hold conversations with more than four different people to be extraordinary successful. Going to events where you hear speaker after speaker applaud being part of this accepting family while you are alone will suck. (Personally, I feel least welcome when there is not enough seating and people have started saving seats for their extended family; that always reminds me how alone I am.)

There is a small minority of people who see single Masters as dangerous outsiders who cannot be trusted. To them, we are no different than the legions of predatory internet dominants who invade the inboxes of innocent slaves. Some may see us as competition, thinking that we are looking to seduce their slaves from their collars, or we will get in the way of them finding more slaves. A lot of this will depend on your gender and orientation; this is how I have felt as a cis heterosexual male dominant, I cannot guarantee that you will be treated better or worse.

Most of the community's resources are aimed at being in this relationship, strengthening it and maintaining it. Thus, there are not a lot of resources available for the single Master to find a slave. When we do have resources, those are often shared with established poly dynamics looking to expand. Unfortunately, I don't think the needs of single Masters correlate with the needs of a poly dynamic, and sometimes I think they get more out of those resources than we do.

Let me be clear: I do not think most of the people in our communities dislike us. I do not believe that these issues are intentional, and I would not bother writing about them if I thought so. Most of the people who enter these communities come in as couples already in a power exchange relationship, or are looking to become that kind of relationship. It might have been decades since some of them were single, and some of them will never be single in this community. I think that if they spent a weekend at a BDSM conference alone where no one knew who they were, they would understand how difficult it can be to hold space here as a single Master, and might think about how to give us the support we need.

These criticisms are not intended to persuade you against being a part of your local community. There are a lot of warm, genuine, intelligent, kind members in these communities. Not only do these communities have the best information for living this lifestyle, but they will promote new ideas for your personal growth. The communities I've been in have tried extremely hard to be inclusive to every type of person, but when they fail to live up to those standards it really hurts, and you should be aware of that. As a single dominant I must acknowledge these issues and let you know that this path will be difficult.

As challenging as it is, it can still be an excellent learning experience and a unique opportunity for personal growth. I believe that being single gives us certain advantages that the coupled members of our community lack. Understand that this is a temporary phase of your life and at some point your bachelorhood will end; it is up to you to decide how you spend your time here.

The best thing about being a single Master is that it gives you ample opportunity to figure out who you are. We have often talked about the importance of figuring out just who we are and what kind of Master we want to be. I think it is harder to figure out who you really are when you are already in a relationship. Slaves, play partners, toys and parties are fun, but they are distractions that take up your time. When you are by yourself, you will find that all you can do is figure out who you are. The times when I have felt alone in this community were the best times to figure out who I was and why I wanted to be in this lifestyle. To give you an example, I have found that I do not really need to do pick-up play or to involve impact play in a possible relationship. I know this because when I have considered what I was craving, pick-up play at public parties was not what that I wanted. I would not have come to this realization if I had constant access to play partners.

You are going to have to see being single as an advantage, not a disadvantage. I think it is particularly important for your mental well-being to look at this stage in your life as an enjoyable moment. The joy of being a single Master is that you are only responsible for yourself; you are free to do what you want! Because I am only responsible for myself, I am free to pursue whatever hobbies, skills or passions that I want and if necessary, abandon them when I feel like it. I am free to change my plans whenever I want and for whatever reason. For example, one day I was out finishing errands and as I got to my car, I saw that it was beginning to rain while the afternoon traffic was picking up. There was a movie theater a block away, so instead of having to deal with the weather and the traffic, I would go see a movie and let it all pass. I did not have to tell anyone that I was changing my plans or worry I was upsetting anyone else's plans. Ultimately, my situation is unique to myself; finding the advantages in your life will require you to be mindful. Look at your life and figure out what you can do that other people may not be able to do, and take pleasure in your privileges. The joy is not in doing whatever you want but in the freedom to do whatever you want.

This is the time if your life to figure out what makes you unique, and what sets you apart from the other Masters in this lifestyle. If we follow the maxim that every Master and slave is different, unique in their own way, then everyone brings something to our lifestyle that no one else can. Figuring this out will, again, require you to figure out who you are, and thankfully as a single Master you will have the time. You will also have to believe that you are special enough to bring something to our community that no one else can. That might be hard to do, as a lot of us have been taught that we are not special … but I believe you are special, glorious reader. If my mad ramblings do not make any sense, at least take away the knowledge that I genuinely believe that you are special, you are worth knowing and you enrich our community by being a part of it.

As a single Master I find it is important to have an outlet for one's dominant feelings, otherwise they are at risk of creative problems. My single greatest enemy of a single Master is going through the motions, getting stuck in the daily routine of life, getting compliant with the safety of familiarity. You might risk being so comfortable with where you are that you decide not to continue pursuing this lifestyle. There is nothing wrong with deciding that this path is no longer right for you, but for me, this is something I crave and I am not yet ready to go back into the closet. If you are like me, you are going to have to fight to keep these desires. You will have to get creative in finding outlets for your dominance. Again, being mindful and knowing who you are will help you find examples. I know this does not sound easy, but nothing worth doing is easy.

A great outlet for single Masters is volunteering, putting your time and energy into the service of your community. When you are new to the community and are having issues fitting in, volunteering is a great opportunity to break that ice. Volunteering for our communities will show that you are committed to their success and longevity. This gives you the opportunity to meet new people and become acquainted with event organizers, and it will mean a lot to know that they find you reliable. (Sometimes hiring a single Master as a volunteer will have advantages over partnered volunteers; we are only on our time schedule, so we do not have to manage our volunteer time with our partner time.) Keep in mind that volunteering will not be a shortcut to finding a slave or being more accepted, but it does feel good and it helps our community.

There are also a lot of volunteering opportunities outside of the M/s community; the rest of the world is just as busy and is just as in need of competent hands. I have always enjoyed volunteering at the local homeless shelters, helping them serve meals to those in need. Serving that community is an outlet for my urge to make a difference, as I service those who are often not served. Taking pride in your volunteer work is a much-needed confidence boost for single Masters; you may not be getting exactly what you need, but you are making the world a better place.

When it comes to finding your slave, I feel that the best advice is to get out there and look. Life is, unfortunately, not like a Japanese animated cartoon; a beautiful slave is not going to just come out of your television or bathroom mirror. You must get out of your house and go places if you want to have any luck at finding that slave. You will have better luck being part of a community where this is accepted, which means going to munches and events and traveling to (sometimes far away) regional conferences. In my experience, online communities just do not provide the type of interactions that you will need to find a good candidate. Some people have had success in finding a partner online and the internet is an amazing tool at connecting like-minded people around the world. There have even been times in my travels when the online communities have been warmer and more accepting than the real-life communities, but I believe that you will get far more out of socializing with the real-world M/s community than you will with internet-based communities. (But your mileage may vary.)

Managing your time is an important aspect if looking for a partner is your first priority. If you find yourself volunteering for a group and it is not giving you opportunities to find a partner, then volunteer elsewhere. If our events are not providing you with opportunities to find a partner, then stop going to those events. If you are not feeling welcome at a group, then find another group. Don't be afraid to spend your time in non-kink related groups, as my experience is that they don't have the same hangups about single people that the M/s community does. You have the right to feel welcome and accepted, and if another group accepts you better than the M/s community, spend your time with them. If you don't feel welcome in a group, let them know; they will not know there is a problem unless we speak up. I believe in our community organizers and I believe they do care about us finding the partners we want. But it might take hearing our voices to get them to start making things happen.

Even if you find that it is difficult finding the slave that you want, do not settle for a less than optimal partner. While the perfect slave is an illusion and every relationship will require compromises, if the foundation of your relationship is based on settling, it will not be a fulfilling relationship. Everyone deserves to have their needs met and I think it's better to let the less-than-optimal partner go find someone who betters fits their needs. You will need to be patient and you will need to believe that the partner you want is out there for you. Also, please be kind to the single slaves who are not compatible with you; they face their own challenges and their path is not any easier than ours.

If the pool of possible partners is too shallow for you, then you will have to find a deeper pool, which means going outside of your local community to find a partner. I believe that there are a lot more people in this world who are interested in authority-based relationships than show up in any community. Getting involved in other communities is a chance to meet more people and increases your chances of finding your preferred partner. I feel this approach is best for single Masters who are a bit more seasoned and knowledgeable than those who are just beginning their journey. Your knowledge will help you come across as more confident and it will show that you take this seriously, which will help attract someone who has only fantasized about having this lifestyle. If you are already carrying a lot of knowledge about this process, you can be the one to show them that it can be a healthy reality.

Remember, fellow single Masters, you are not alone. You are not the only lonely Master afraid they will never have a slave. There are a lot more of us out there than you see and there are a thousand more who gave up. Remember that this is just a temporary phase of your life; at some point your bachelorhood will end and you will enter another stage of your journey. When that time comes, do not forget the rest of us. Good luck out there and stand proud.

───────────◗●◖───────────

*John Anderson Orr, known as Bannor in the kink community, is a heterosexual dominant Leatherman living in Columbia, South Carolina. He is a graduate of the House of Decorum's Leather M/s Mentorship Program and the MTTA Academy Master Weekend class #29. He can be found at the Master slave Conference or wherever a Street Fighter Third Strike arcade cabinet can be found.*

# Learning To Lean In

*Andrew James*

In early 2016, our family took a trip from our home in Massachusetts to California. We caught up with friends in the Bay Area, then flew down to Disneyland and had a grand time. On the plane home, I felt like I was coming down with something, and by the time we landed, I had a fever and chills.

It's not unusual to pick up a bug when traveling, but I didn't get better. After many weeks I was still exhausted, barely able to get out of bed, and every muscle in my body ached. Ten months and dozens of vials of blood later, a rheumatologist diagnosed me with fibromyalgia, a neurological condition that causes chronic muscle pain, brain fog, and a host of other nasty symptoms.

This was not the first time I had faced a serious illness, but my previous experiences had been of the mental, not physical, variety. When it comes to depression, I am a battle-hardened warrior. There, the trick is to stay alive for a few weeks until the meds kick in and the fog lifts enough for me to benefit from the next round of psychotherapy. Although it doesn't feel like it during those dark weeks, my depression will eventually ease. I know that from long experience.

So does my girl, Anne. During our almost 25-year marriage, more than eight of which have been spent in a 24/7 authority dynamic, she has seen me through multiple bouts of Major Depressive Disorder. We have protocols in place for the times when the darkness descends and I tell her that, despite my love for her, I no longer believe life is worth living. We both know that it's depression whispering those poisonous words in my ear. There's a temporary disconnect between what I know and what I feel, a wire loose in my brain. She moves quickly: sharp things disappear from the kitchen and even seemingly innocuous pills vanish from the medicine chest. Calls are made, appointments scheduled, prescriptions picked up. Because she does these things with practiced efficiency, I know that I can trust her with my life, and with my truth, however confused and painful. Eventually, the psych meds will do their job, and I will emerge from the suffocating gray cocoon of depression to find my girl, concerned but strong, waiting for me.

Fibromyalgia is different. There is no cure. Although some people do go into remission—or discover that a more temporary condition, such as post-viral syndrome, was really the culprit in the first place—most people will live with it for the rest of their days. Fibro does not respond to treatment the way that chemical depression does. The medications typically prescribed have side effects that range from annoying to debilitating in themselves. Practices like tai chi and water therapy can help, assuming you're well enough to do them in the first place. For most of 2016 and 2017, I wasn't.

Like many people who face a devastating diagnosis, I grieved for what I had lost: ease of movement, refreshing sleep, social connection, travel plans made on the assumption that hiking around southern France would cause no more trouble than a few blisters or a sunburn. I denied, I raged, I bargained. As my horizons contracted, so did my heart. I no longer shared it with my girl. It became a tender, bruised thing to be protected at all costs, even from the person I love the most.

As the months dragged on, my illness began to take a serious toll, not just on me, but also on Anne. My girl's primary love language is physical touch, and on my worst days, I could barely stand the feel of a bed sheet on my skin, let alone a human hand. Chronic pain sapped my libido, and even when I was game, there was no guarantee my body would cooperate for long enough for either of us to experience the pleasure we craved. Eventually, I gave up trying. As a result, Anne shut down sexually as well.

Although she had promised to stand by me "in sickness and in health," becoming the caregiver for a disabled M-type was especially hard for her. As a preteen, Anne had been forced into the caregiver role for a domineering, abusive parent who developed a debilitating chronic illness. To this day, she lives with complex PTSD as a result of the abuse she suffered at that person's hands. Because these experiences happened when she was so young, she wasn't able to distinguish between her parent's physical illness and the underlying personality disorder that was the source of the abusive behavior. Although she knew in her heart that I had nothing at all in common with her abuser, taking care of an authority figure who was stuck in bed with a chronic condition that caused mobility and cognitive issues was one enormous trauma trigger.

As I shrank further and further into my shell, I left her adrift, without the protection, guidance, and care that are my role in our dynamic. When she got up the courage to tell me that she couldn't feel my dominance anymore, I became defensive and resentful. I didn't want to hear that I wasn't doing my job as an M-type when getting out of bed long enough to shower represented a major achievement. I was barely able to keep my own life in order, let alone direct hers. Couldn't she see that?

Beneath those emotional reactions lay a sea of self-doubt. Could I really be an effective M-type in my condition? What did it mean to be in charge when I was physically dependent on another person? Would my girl eventually tire of playing nursemaid—a role neither of us could manage to eroticize, despite our best efforts—and leave me for an able-bodied dominant who could better meet her emotional and sexual needs?

We were at an impasse. With the help of peer counseling and a short but intense round of couples therapy, we were able to find a way through. That way required me to own up to my own failures as an M-type. (Anne did her own work, but that is not my story to tell.)

First, I had to admit that I had been focusing on myself, not on Anne or our relationship. There is something to be said for putting on your own oxygen mask first, but that advice works best in emergencies, not as a general directive. There's also a difference between the kind of mutually agreeable "selfishness" that M-types express in a consensual dynamic and the unhealthily myopic self-involvement of a person who can't see past their own pain. As an M-type, I bear the responsibility for both the direction of the relationship as a whole and for my girl's well-being on a day-to-day level. By allowing myself to wallow in self-pity—something that runs counter to my sense of personal honor—I let those responsibilities fall by the wayside. In short, I stopped acting as the M-type I had agreed to be.

Second, I tried to "Lone Ranger" it, to be a rock and an island, rather than graciously and gratefully accepting the service that my girl offered. My girl is not service-oriented in the way that some s-types are;

she doesn't get off on simply being useful. But she is profoundly *me*-oriented, and she was determined to serve me to the best of her ability. I did not acknowledge—or often, I'm ashamed to admit, even notice—the many acts of service she performed for me during the worst of my illness. I allowed my resentment about being sick to become resentment of my need for help, and with it, resentment of her service role.

Third, I got caught in the trap of trying to live up to an internal stereotype of dominance. I had a vision in my head of what a "real Dominant" was, and it did not include being chronically ill or dependent on my girl for practical, unsexy things like refilling my med minder or driving me to physical therapy appointments. (Never mind that some of the M/s couples I admire most are in exactly this situation; internalized ableism is as insidious as any infectious disease.) I needed to retool my self-image by rejecting the cardboard cut-out that lived in my head—I call him "Master DomlyPants"—and owning a more authentic expression of dominance, which in my case is the Daddy archetype.

What I learned from this experience, and what I want to share with readers of this book, is a deceptively simple idea: **When the going gets rough, lean in.** Lean into the relationship. Lean into your role. Lean into the structure you've built together. If possible, create *more* structure, not less. If you do need to ease up on your protocols for a time, choose a few key practices that clearly reaffirm and reinforce your dynamic and perform them daily, without fail. These do not need to be grand gestures. One of ours is to bookend our days with a morning affirmation and an evening moment of gratitude. Both rituals take seconds to perform, but the effects ripple out into our days and buoy us up when we're foundering.

I am happy to report that I am currently in good health. While I am not entirely pain-free, my fibromyalgia is manageable and significant flares are now rare. My doctor has used the word "remission." I'll take it.

But more important is the fact that my relationship is healthier than ever. By taking responsibility for my failures and missteps during the worst of my illness, I've become a better and more trustworthy M-type for my s-type. I have learned to take seriously the promises I make every morning in our affirmation ritual: to protect and guide and care for my girl.

As I write this, we are in the midst of a global pandemic. When my girl and I shut the doors to the outside world to keep ourselves and our community safe, we leaned in. It may be the end of the world as we know it, but we feel fine.

*Andrew James (they/them and he/him) is a genderqueer, transmasculine Daddy who writes and teaches about consensual Dominant/submissive relationships as an avenue for personal and spiritual growth. They are the author of six books on alternative relationships and sexuality, including Erotic Slavehood (as Christina Abernathy) and The Way of the Pleasure Slave. AJ has been involved in the D/s and kink communities since 1992. They and their wife, Anne, have been together for almost 25 years and have been in a 24/7 authority-transfer dynamic since 2012. They can be found at HeartofDs.com.*

# I Am Crunchy Peanut Butter: The Problem of Consistency

*Raven Kaldera*

The title of this piece is from a joke I heard tossed out by a bunch of very intelligent and thoughtful slaves who were just coming out of a support group meeting for people on the s-side of the slash. "We like our masters like we like our peanut butter—with uniform consistency!" And then my slaveboy glanced at me and piped up, "Well, I've learned to be good with the crunchy variety too, over time."

That was several years into our dynamic, and that point was a long time coming; we'd both worked hard for it. I'll scrap the metaphor now and talk about consistency—in one's actions, in one's reliability, in one's views and values. Slaves and submissives are in vulnerable positions. Anyone who puts themselves on the bottom end of an unequal relationship is in a vulnerable position, and if it's emotionally intimate, they are much more so. When you have less recourse than the person above you, it becomes very important to know what to expect, and what is expected of you. It's hard enough to be the person with less power. Having the person with more power be erratic and unreliable can be terrifying.

I understand that problem on a deep level, actually. I grew up in a highly dysfunctional family with two mentally ill parents. I know viscerally what it is to be in the power of extremely erratic people, when you can never count on anything to be what it's been promised to be. I learned to dodge and shift and duck and adapt and make do. I learned to be hypervigilant, to always be checking for the blow coming seemingly out of nowhere, the support suddenly pulled out from under you. I learned to believe that the Universe was an uncertain place where you could never count on anything. Instead of slowly and painstakingly building a life with a solid foundation under it, I concentrated on learning to slalom around the oncoming storms.

Of course, when I got my slaveboy, my life wasn't entirely without solid foundations. I'd become a parent years before that, and the presence of children means the necessity for at least some kind of solid foundation. (Although I fear that I probably wasn't the most consistent of parents.) I had a home, a career, a solid primary relationship with my egalitarian partner. (We are polyamorous, as is my slaveboy, but that's not relevant to this essay.) The bills got paid, the necessities were covered, we weren't well off but we were surviving reasonably well. My life was not a dumpster fire. I had a good sense of myself, who I was, what I valued and didn't value. I had social capital, friends and tribe. I thought that I was solid enough to offer a good anchor for a full-time Master/slave relationship.

However, my slaveboy turned out to be someone who needs much stronger consistency than I'd ever built into my life. We have a hundred things in common, but that one thing stood out as a major difference. Some of that is his neurological issues, but honestly I've heard this complaint from all sorts of s-types, so it seems to be a rather common beginner M/s stumbling block. The dance we did would end up like this:

1) We come up with a protocol, or a rule, or a ritual. It looked, on the surface, to be something that would be highly rewarding for both of us. Maybe it would solve a problem we'd been having with some process. Maybe it touched us emotionally, reminded us of who we are. Maybe it was just hot. We'd decide to implement it.

2) He'd forget to do it, probably sometime in the first couple of weeks. He's human, he's got issues remembering things due to neurological problems, it would fall off of his plate.

3) I'd forget that he was supposed to be doing it, so I didn't notice when it stopped happening.

4) He'd realize that it had fallen off his plate and he hadn't been doing it for … well, sometimes a week or two, or even longer. He'd also realized that I hadn't said anything.

5) He'd freak out. The fact that I Hadn't Even Noticed was clear proof that I didn't care. How could I expect him to get this right without any oversight, he would cry. There would be recriminations and tears and I would be the Worst Master Ever.

6) I, of course, wanted to do my part right as well. I'm a reasonable human being and I acknowledge when I've made an error, and I

try to fix the problem. (M-types are often fix-it types who want to make things better, and it's hard when we can't.) I'd try harder to remember it. The problem is that "try harder" may be an adequate Plan B, but it is a completely inadequate Plan C and a terrible Plan D. I had to do more than try harder. I had to make hard decisions.

Later, I got to talk to other power exchange couples, and I discovered that what I'd considered my own failing was actually very common—at least half of the masters I spoke to had gone through the same problem. One told an amusing story of a decision that his slave would meet him at the door, posed in a certain way, and that she would wait for him to release her. That lasted about a week, and then he had a particularly difficult day at work and blew right past his posed slave, grumbling. As soon as he'd taken off his coat and settled himself in a chair, he realized that she was nowhere to be seen and called her. "Where are you, slave?" "I'm here, Master, waiting for you to release me!" she called from where she was stuck in her pose by the door.

It's especially tempting to assume, when this sort of thing happens repeatedly, that it is evidence of the failure of the power dynamic—that the two of you will not be able to pull it off. Please don't look at it like that. It's just a problem to be handled; it doesn't mean that the two of you can't manage in an unequal relationship.

After several such mistakes, my slaveboy and I went into problem-solving mode. Eventually we came up with a multi-pronged approach to the problem, which I'll delineate below.

### 1) Everything Is An Experiment.

We learned to approach each new potential rule or protocol or ritual as an experiment. Maybe we could do it, maybe we couldn't—and no matter how awesome it looked to be, no matter how disappointing its failure would make one or both of us, we made a commitment not to get broken up about anything in the experimental stage. If it went sideways, we would troubleshoot, brainstorm, and problem-solve, trying a different slant to see if it could still work in some other form. If it continued to fail, we agreed that it just wasn't going to work for our lives, and let go of it.

## 2) The Annoyance Factor.

We took a hard look at the rules, protocols, and rituals that actually worked—not so much where my slaveboy remembered to do them without fail, as ones where I reliably noticed when he wasn't doing them and pointed it out. They all had one quality in common— what I call the Annoyance Factor. If the lack of his action caused me fairly immediate annoyance, I'd notice and do something about it. While we didn't want to cause me more annoyance than necessary in my daily life, if it was easy to build in a mild annoyance factor, we did. It made for a much higher rate of conscious supervision.

## 3) The Slave Is A Tool.

Do I forget to give him regular positive acknowledgment for his service? Then he can be ordered to come find me whenever he feels in need of it and ask, in a way I find pleasant. It's often possible to use the s-type as a tool to make things easier for the M-type to cope, if you're creative about it. Some s-types may feel put out by this, but they need to be reminded that it's better than having it just fall off the plate all the time. Another example might be that if we're starting on a new rule and I'm afraid that I will lose track of it, he can set up an email reminder for me that comes in every few days: "Sir, are there any new slave behaviors that you should be checking on?" Which brings us to the next rule:

## 4) Technology Is Your Friend.

Use shared online calendars. Use online programs that will send reminders to one or both people on the schedule they set up. You can have your s-type do the research and find anything out there which might help for mutual reminders. Don't get bogged down in feelings of "We should just be able to remember this! We shouldn't need help!" Take the help and get some sleep. If you find that you don't need it later, when things are more settled, you can always discontinue it. However, we've found that while some rules settle in and become second nature, we keep thinking of new ones as Life throws us more fresh curve balls, so we keep resorting to them.

*5) Variable Reward Schedule.*

This is a fairly complex concept, so bear with me. In tests on both animals and humans, behaviorists discovered that if a reward comes every time and then suddenly doesn't come, the recipient gets angry and stops trying. (Think of a vending machine. If you put your money in and nothing happens, you usually don't keep putting money in. You assume that it's broken, because your past experiences have been money in = stuff coming out. You might even kick the machine or complain to the owner.) However, behaviorists found that if the rewards don't come out every time, the recipient keeps trying to get them. They expect it to be variable, but they also expect that it will come on at least a semi-regular basis. (Think of a slot machine, as opposed to that vending machine. How much money do people drop into slot machines without getting anything back?)

Of course, the rewards do actually have to come frequently enough to make it worth their while, or both animals and humans will give up and wander off. Also, when you are first starting out with a behavior, if you want consistent results, you do need to pony up consistent rewards, if only the reward of paying attention and showing that you care about the behavior appearing. However, once the s-type has mastered the behavior, you can skip a reward—and then start again the next time. Slowly, make the rewards less consistent, but know your s-type well enough to know how often they have to come to keep them motivated.

If you institute a variable rewards system, you cut yourself slack. It means that periodic dropping of balls won't be such a painful thing for the s-type, because they're used to it, and—more important than any reward—*they know what to expect, and they know what is expected of them.* On the other hand, if the feedback stops entirely, that's not good, so back it up with other tools such as the ones above.

In addition, if you insist on the slave enacting a super-strict and fairly difficult regular protocol—one that takes a great deal of their focus and energy, where it's hard for them to relax—it's better to stick with consistent rewards. The same goes for a temporary situation where they are having to really struggle due to outside circumstances. The harder their situation is, the more frequently they need to see that the M-type is invested in their process. Remember that the M-type's involvement with any aspect of the s-type's process is a powerful impetus for them to keep paying attention to it, while if it's clear that the M-type doesn't give a damn about it, that can often be a powerful impetus for letting it slack off.

This problem is neither easy nor trivial, but it's possible to put systems in place to make it work more skillfully. Patience with each other is important. In fact, that's something the M-type can mandate—"We're going to be patient and generous with each other through all of this." Of course, that means the M-type has to model exactly those qualities of patience and generosity when it comes to the s-type forgetting the new action. If an attitude is to be a team effort, the M-type needs to be in the forefront of demonstrating it. That's why my email notes that say, "Are there any new slave behaviors that you should be checking on?" usually also come with a line below saying, "Remember to be patient, generous, and compassionate!" so I can breathe and get my head together before diving into the supervisory capacity.

Remember also that although all M-types make mistakes, it's better to acknowledge them and start the cleanup immediately, rather than trying to hide them. S-types watch us closely anyway—it's how they figure out our preferences, or at least the ones we've forgotten to tell them about—and they will notice eventually, and then even more trust will be lost. (Trust me on this one, I've made this mistake enough that I cringe, remembering those days.) When the M-type makes a mistake, it's scary for the s-type. However, if the M-type shows that even though mistakes are inevitable, they will saddle up and find a path out of the muddle one way or another, the s-type will come to trust that much more realistic promise. And that's a consistency that even the crunchy peanut butter types can learn to achieve.

# From Feral Dominance to Competent Mastery
*Unbennes, owner of caeth*

### Feral Dominance and Owning Ownership

Love is our foundation; deep, abiding love, the kind that outlasts infatuation then continues to sustain, decade after decade. Master/slave is a relationship structure that works for us. It is less necessary than the love, as we know from having been together for 29 years before moving to that structure, and yet M/s has served us well in the years since 2007.

I will not reiterate the full story of the origins of caeth's and my relationship, as it can be found in my chapter in *Paradigms of Power* (Alfred Press, 2014). Suffice it to say that when we committed to 24/7 M/s, I had no idea what I was doing.

At the time he and I met in 1978, I was what I now call a "feral dominant". I had not done the introspection to be able to articulate that, though I believe that all individuals have value, they vary in strengths and weaknesses, introversion and extroversion, tendency to dominate or to submit. I had a sense of entitlement at odds with both my egalitarian values and my underprivileged history. I went through the world expecting to have my way most of the time, and somehow people mostly gave it to me. Perhaps because of that frequent wordless compliance, perhaps because of the vestiges of effects from being abused, I have always had a difficult time actively asking for what I want. Owning my dominance showed me that paradox, and I am still working on that issue.

When we met, caeth was submissive, whether or not he thought of it that way at the time. His fantasy was to serve women. He was also very, *very* compatible with me. He was careful and gentle with me as I healed from the traumas of abuse and rape. Over time, he requested play in which I topped him. I was afraid to do it, because I did not want to become a monster like those who abused me had been. With him, I learned that I was allowed to have my own limits; that I could provide him what he craved when it suited me, and that I could stop when I wanted to. I thought of it as consensual play that lived in its own box tucked under the bed except when in use. Though we were still ostensibly egalitarian, I was blind to the fact that I had become *de facto* dominant in many areas of our relationship until I owned it, after I offered 24/7 M/s to him.

### Misconceptions and Overcoming Them

I had plenty of misconceptions!

First, I thought 24/7 M/s meant that I would have to deliver kink 24/7. In reality, M/s means that I get to retain control of whether, when, and how we do kinky play. If I don't want it, it doesn't happen. Since our M/s is founded on love, and I am adamant about consent, our relationship is built on mutual agreements and ongoing tacit consent.

Again, I was afraid that I would become an abusive monster. The adage "power corrupts" haunted me. Acknowledging a different definition of power helped me immensely. "Power is the rate at which work gets done" comes from physics. What I have is authority, including authority over his power to get work done for me. Authority I could handle, having been a parent and a teacher for years. My sense of honor, my love for him, and my self-control are what reined me away from abusive or monstrous behavior. Because I was so scared that I thought I would run away from M/s or go into denial about it, I promised that I would not back out unless that was what he wanted. I did spend some time in denial, but I got over it.

Patience helped too. When he wanted to try e-stim, it terrified me. At first, I said "hell no", but the more it sat there not happening, the more I felt it was my fear running the show instead of me. I wrapped my brain around it, and we tried it. It's not so terrible close up, realizing that it is still me deciding what and how much would happen. This served me very well when I broke my shoulder and e-stim was used to relieve my pain after physical therapy sessions.

I also feared that that if I couldn't become a standard issue dominatrix, someone might take him away from me; that he would be lured away by a stiletto-heeled vixen. It turned out that, just as I didn't want "a" slave, mindlessly obedient to all the orders I didn't want to give, he didn't want just "a" Mistress. He wanted, specifically, *me*. He wanted the security of feeling owned *by me*.

Another misconception I had was that others might try to dictate to me how to be his Mistress. I thought that there were universally recognized rules, and that I would have to micro-manage even though that thought was overwhelming.

Although I was adamant that I wasn't going to own him the way someone else dictated, reading others' works helped me figure out what my own way looked like. Though the balance of our power is no longer equal, he didn't lose his brains in the process, and since I have always highly appreciated his intelligence, I codified that I would not only request but sometimes demand his input into my considerations when making decisions.

Since he, as my slave, could not dictate to me what I wanted, I had to do a lot of introspection, while he did a lot of observation. We talked, but we also wrote stuff down, and then chose what parts of that stuff to show to each other. We wrote notes back on what the other had written. We held papers in our hands through some rough conversations, while the papers literally got tearstained. We held onto each other. We started and finished with the base assumption that we love each other and both want things to work. I asked him to do research, and filter out the stuff that would trigger me, which helped a fair amount too.

I remember asking him about various M/s tropes with the phrasing, "I don't think I necessarily want this, but what are your thoughts about _____?" This got us able to talk about subjects that could then be shelved when they turned out not to be of interest to either of us. Knowing they were shelved by the two of us together made them easier to let go of.

Some things I made standing orders, other things he offered as anticipatory service. Even so, there are still times when caeth is frustrated by my not articulating what it is that I want. What is more difficult for us is when he wants a firm decision to be made about something in which I am not invested or feel ambivalent. In those situations, he has to put up with feeling exasperated.

This brings us to another common misconception which we, fortunately, didn't have. We understood that M/s contracts are not legally binding. They can, however, be emotionally and psychologically binding, and the negotiation process can be valuable, especially for folks who do their thinking in writing. It took us about a year to figure out what works best for us. We each have as much say as we want, because I want input from him so that the best possible decision can be made, and he wants me to be served and for the final authority to be mine. We call our agreement documents our "Dragon Taming Manual". We pledged an Oath of Fealty to each other that clarified and deepened our bond.

### Relationship Bumps and Smaller Mistakes

We struggled at first with the concepts of service and obedience. In our early days of M/s, when caeth was balky for what seemed to me to be trivial reasons, I said, "Do you want to do this, or don't you?" It was not effective communication. I prefer cooperation and reasoning to saying, "Because I said so!"

A lot of what we read went on about how "a real slave always obeys". The expected response to disobedience ranged from punishment to breaking up, and breaking up is not on the table. I don't like to punish anyway, but one of the punishments I used backfired massively. Our M/s was in limbo after that big bump. We spent about three days mulling over what we were going to do about the shattered trust. Rather than end the M/s, we came to the conclusion that punishment as a whole just doesn't work well for us. I had to balance between giving him the firmness that he needed and feeling abject and guilty about having fucked up so badly. We worked together to rebuild the trust.

Neither of us wants to abandon the other. Even so, abandonment issues were at the heart of our second big bump. We were asked to help a friend make a music video in San Francisco, near Fisherman's Wharf, on a Saturday during tourist season. Naturally, parking was abysmal. To add to the challenge, there was a wedding being held in the hotel nearest to Ghirardelli Square, so their huge parking structure was completely full. I told caeth to get out of the car and walk to the video venue, and that I would go park the car and join him as soon as I could. Mind you, he is an introvert, hates crowds, hates unfamiliar places, hates San Francisco, and wasn't entirely certain of where to go. By the time I got back to him and we went to work in the video, he was a mess. Fortunately for us, looking miserable was not inappropriate to the role.

Again, we were in limbo for a few days, with him working through whether he could continue to consent to being mine when I had put him into such a situation. I did what I could to ease him, and he chose to continue with the M/s. I decided that even if it was less convenient, I would henceforth err on the side of keeping him beside me. Where others might have said, "suck it up", I recognize that he is a very sensitive and delicate instrument. One would not use a Stradivarius to pound in a nail.

In both cases, my approach to fixing the issues started with, "Well, we won't do *that* again." The trick to making it work is in correctly identifying what *that* is, and addressing its underlying causes as well as steering clear of a particular behavior.

Minor issues arose when others chose to start giving him orders after having observed him doing as I say. One of the times this happened, I informed the person that he was taking instructions from me but was not available for her to give orders. On another occasion, we were doing yardwork together, and caeth was diverted from my goal by a neighbor with their own agenda. That manipulation was more subtle. I ended up not defending the boundary but instead withdrawing our participation. He is mine, not anyone else's.

I have learned that he is such a perfectionist that leaving him a list of things to do while I am gone is actually dangerous. When I said "Clean my fencing rapiers," he interpreted it as "Polish to a mirror sheen," not "Get the rust off and the dings softened." Because I wasn't there to clarify, he grew angry as he worked, and it took me a while to bring him back to where we both wanted him to be. I had to show him what my expectations were, and make him stop at "good enough", no matter how much it offended his perfectionism. He has adjusted to some of my "lower standards", so we can be more relaxed about those things.

It's worst when one of us mishears the other and makes wrong assumptions, or when one of us phrases something very badly and it gets interpreted as meaning the opposite thing from what we were trying to say. I can't remember a single time when getting things straightened out didn't show us to be pretty much aligned rather than perpendicular or opposed. We often can't prevent mishearing or bad phrasing, but we do persist in communicating until the misconceptions are cleared away and the "floor swept".

I have come to realize that I don't place obedience at a very high priority. He can balk and second guess. He can protest. He can say "no". He can ignore my orders. If it's an order I care about, I will work with him to get compliance. More often, it's in the nature of a casual request. If I don't enforce it, it's because I don't care enough to do so. He's still my slave. He is my slave until and unless he says, "I can't do this anymore. I withdraw my consent."

Nowadays, when he resists, we talk about why the resistance is there, and address the underlying issue. Sometimes I'm a bit of an ass and it takes a while to fix things. Since our M/s includes his right to rescind consent, we work to keep our relationship structure one in which we both want to participate.

What do I do now when I'm wrong? 1 First: Apologize. Second: Communicate. Third: Make a decision. Not only is apologizing when one screws up not a sign of weakness, it is a sign of strength.

### Training and Other Fetishes

We played for a while with "slave training", but I got bored with it. We found that kneeling hurts his knees, so he is only allowed to do it rarely, and preferably on a pillow. We added a few things to our very low protocols, and abandoned the rest. I didn't want him to become a different person, so we didn't need to do a lot of training. He did take a class so he can put art on my latte. He does hearts, flowers, and sometimes ferns. He studied how to give manicures and pedicures because I hate having strangers touch my feet, and I was not up to doing my own nail care after having had my surgeries. He taught himself how to make chainmaille when I wanted a glove. I value these things more than downcast eyes or artificial speech patterns.

While it makes a lovely fantasy, it is not practical for us that caeth be naked 24/7. For one thing, he earns the income and going to work requires clothing. For another, I like to have him with me out in the world. It would drive both of us nuts if he were stuck at home naked when I wanted to be out. He does work naked in the back yard, but has to wear shorts where the neighbors will see because I don't want to squick them. They have not consented to being part of our dynamic.

I defend his boundaries around his job. Years before M/s, his bosses had him working in crunch mode so hard that he ended up getting pneumonia. I called them up and gave them an earful. Now he has to ask my permission to work overtime. I can also keep him home from work or even tell him to quit. They only get to rent his brilliance. I own it. But again, I not only know which side my bread is buttered on, I like having that butter available to me. Fortunately, I rarely need to meddle with his job.

I have been asked, "How do you keep things fresh and exciting? How do you avoid stagnation?" As I am over 60, "fresh and exciting" has lost some of its appeal while the appeal of "sustaining and comfortable" has increased. Richness has superseded freshness as our priority. It's possible to have some stillness without stagnation. We continue learning and growing, but our growth is now more like an old tree, getting broader rather than taller.

## Conclusion

From time to time we do specifically and openly discuss whether this framework is still working for us, and it has continued to do so since 2007.

I am his master in that I hold authority over him, and exert it as serves our relationship. Because he belongs to me, he is strengthened by knowing he need not submit to anyone else. He finds this very liberating. Bonds that don't chafe are still bonds. My mastery is in the art of owning him competently.

———————————————

*Unbennes has used this name since April of 2008, when she followed caeth onto FetLife, a year into their M/s dynamic, and 28 years into their marriage. She is an Elder Witch, a writer, a teacher and sometime counselor, a grandma, and a designer and Maker in several media. She lives in a forest in California, not too far from the ocean.*

# Tips for Helping Self-Esteem in an S-type

*Raven Kaldera*

One of the many negative myths generated about power dynamic relationships is that the subordinate partner is there because they have terrible self-esteem … because why else would anyone willingly choose to be in a subordinate position? This type of circular reasoning is, of course, false as a general rule. However, that does not change the fact that a certain percentage of s-types do struggle with low self-esteem, just like a certain percentage of egalitarian people—and, for that matter, a certain percentage of dominant types as well. Low self-esteem is the psychological equivalent of the common cold in our society. So, given that, some dominant/master-types are going to end up with s-types whose self-esteem is not so great. And, because so often We Want To Fix Things, of course we want to fix that, too.

The vast majority of M-types do not want a "worthless worm", regardless of the porn. We want competent human beings who are proud to be in our service. This may make an s-type with low self-esteem feel that they aren't even worthy of offering themselves, and they may gravitate to the few who do want "worthless worms" because "obviously those dominants who want strong, competent people wouldn't want me." This doesn't have to be the case, though. And if that new s-type who is sitting adoringly at your feet turns out to have somewhat damaged self-worth, how do you fix it?

This is a list of techniques that have had good results for me. Obviously not every technique is going to work for every s-type; they're all different people. But if any of these techniques help, it will be worth writing them down.

1) First and most important, work hard on getting your s-type to internalize your judgment as being the voice they should follow, even when you're not there. Every s-type has a "master puppet" in their head. It may or may not have traits and qualities that are based on that of a realistic human being. That aside, however, your job is to slowly replace that puppet with a puppet that looks like you, and speaks in your voice, and gives them the advice you would give them. This is a

long, slow process and won't happen overnight, but it is crucial. You want to give them the equivalent of an automatic "WWMS"—What Would Master Say—bracelet. Once you've done that, you can reinforce the fact that *you say they are worthy, and it's your opinion that matters*. They can't argue with that opinion without owning the fact that their internal voice is more important and valid to them than you are. If this isn't working yet, you need to work more on that internal master puppet, through other means.

2) Second, if this is a long-term committed relationship, it can help to tie their self-esteem to how well they please you. Both my boys have large parts of their self-esteem tied to being my good boy. Being proud to be your good s-type, and proud to be in your service, can slowly spread over time to other areas of their life. Really. I promise. But to make this work effectively, you need to show your pleasure. Not just pats on the head and "Good girl" or "Good boy", but "Wow, this is awesome!" "Well, look at you!" "Have I mentioned lately how great it is to have a slave who can make baklava?" and so forth. Pleasing you needs to be a top priority for them. Encourage this. Then, eventually, they will value pleasing you more than valuing their internal negative voice … and because they know that it would please you for them to work on their self-esteem, they will be more motivated to do it.

3) Third, find areas in which they can excel, and push them toward excellence in those areas. One of the things that builds self-esteem, even in an s-type, is "mastery experiences". By this I mean being able to achieve something they didn't think they could achieve. This is a technique much lauded by masters of disabled slaves—find an area that is not trashed by their disability, and push them to excel in that area. (Even when a disabled s-type is so bad off they can't get out of bed, they can still work on giving their M-type accurate and honest self-assessments, being cooperative when the M-type tells them ways to take care of themself, and having a good, cheerful, smiling attitude when the M-type comes up to check on them.) It's important to stress the difference between perfection and excellence. Perfection is irrelevant. Excellence is achievable—and stress also that it is your standard, not theirs, which decides what is excellent.

4) When you push them toward excellence in these areas, look them in the eye and tell them that you believe in them. You believe that they can do this thing. You will be there to help them do it, if they need help, but you have a rock-solid belief in their ability to pull it off if they put their minds to it. (Start with something you really are quite realistically sure they can do—it's not good to set them up for failure on the first few times you try this.) After this has worked a few times, they will internalize your belief in them. To paraphrase one slave who mentioned this: "I believe what he believes, and he believes in me."

5) An exercise I really like: Order them to tell you three good things about themselves. Even small things. Don't let them leave until it's done, and done right. Next time, three other good things about themselves. Do not accept anything phrased in a self-deprecating manner. Make them say it again, more proudly, or at least more matter-of-factly, if necessary. A variation of this works well for depressed s-types—"Tell me three good things about your life!" or "Tell me three good things about me."

6) In that vein, get them checked for neurochemical problems. Depression or other issues of bad brain soup can set up a fog of negativity that nothing can penetrate. If they need medical help, see that they get it, or you're battering yourself against something bigger than you. If they need therapy, see that they get it. Be patient and understand that it's going to take longer if they are constantly being sabotaged by their own brain chemistry—even when you're medicated, the medication doesn't always work, and years of bad brain soup can set up patterns that take a long time to change. This is really another whole issue, but it's something to rule out or try to fix.

7) A somewhat dangerous tool, but one that can work with an s-type who is strongly sexual and finds it easy to eroticize weird things: If there are specific and unchangeable qualities that are the pivot-points of their self-esteem issues, see if there are ways that these qualities can be played with during sex or scenes which eroticize something about them. Perhaps it's eroticizing that quality, perhaps it's eroticizing embarrassment around that quality, perhaps it's eroticizing the master's use of that quality. This does not mean something as clumsy as yelling triggering insults during sex (unless you've both negotiated

experimenting with that). This needs to be done very much as a team, perhaps trying it out with sexy storytelling first before enacting it. However, it can totally turn around an s-type's attitude toward a specific obstacle. "Hey, that obstacle's kind of hot, or weirdly desirable, y'know?" "Wow, I never thought of that!" Again, this won't work for all obstacles or all s-types, but it is a legitimate tool for the right s-type in the right situation.

8) Finally, set up a discipline of stopping internal negative self-talk. Have mantras that they can say when that voice starts. One of the best ways to slowly silence that voice entirely over time is to just never let it speak. Perhaps a good starting mantra could be, "Master says that I am worthy, and I trust them," said to cut off every time the nasty voice starts up in the head. Ask them, at the end of the day, how many times they used that mantra to cut the voice off. Praise them for doing it, even if they only remembered to do it after fifteen minutes of writhing under their own self-torment. Eventually it will become not just a discipline but a habit.

# The Hard Path Walked

*A jointly written piece by Alpha Pup and Boi Nik*

My boi and I have only been together a short time. They are the first slave I've owned and so every day I strive to learn and to be the best Alpha that I can be to them. Since this is my first time on the left side of the slash, you might think I'd be the last person to judge mistakes or pass on advice on potential do's and do not's for other Masters. However, I feel what does give me knowledge to pass on is not my short time as Alpha to my boi; it is in fact from my fifteen years on the right side of the slash, and from my eleven years as an owned slave to my own Master and Husband before his passing in 2015.

Eleven years in service to one person is a long time to make a million mistakes together. Eleven years in service to one person is also a long time to learn just a few tricks and workarounds for some of the difficulties these mistakes may cause.

Much like myself, my Master had once been an owned slave, but in meeting me, he felt called by the need to serve that he saw in me. The two of us had been dating as two slaves for some six months before he decided to ask for release from his then-Master in order to collar me as his slave. When all this came about, it was news to me. I had no idea about his plans. There had been no negotiations, no discussions, no planning of what a dynamic between the two of us might look like. I was young and had no idea such things existed. He told me one day I was now his slave and in my youthful desire to be owned, I accepted that this was all it took.

With my boi, I learned from this experience. I learned the importance of discussions, of negotiations, of making the lists and checking them twice so that both of us would know what we were entering into. As with many things, my boi and I were of the same mind. After we spoke about it, they wrote the below:

> I genuinely agree that taking time in which to negotiate thoroughly a new dynamic is one of the more important things for a beginner Master to be mindful of. I have been in more than one situation where mutual eagerness to progress deeper into a new dynamic has resulted in my attempting to please a Master without having enough information to know how to please that Master.

*From those experiences, I would not seek a Master who was just as susceptible as I to acting, and making decisions, from excitement. I would suggest, instead, they show enough restraint to offer an extended negotiation period, where each person has the time to deeply learn the other.*

*The beginning of the dynamic with my Alpha and I was several weeks long, with a number of vanilla dates as we both got to know each other as people and also shared what we each wanted out of a dynamic, to see if we were logically as compatible as our feelings were making us believe.*

Knowing that my boi and I have the same values, kinks, mindsets and goals for a dynamic makes, I believe, for the best opportunity for a long term, happy, holistic and loving dynamic.

In all of our eleven years together, my Master and I, I can't recall a time when I was ever punished. I don't believe I am perfect, so therefore I am certain there were times when I probably should have been. In looking back, I am quite able to see the times when he became frustrated with me. In these times, he would simply remove himself emotionally from the dynamic, leaving me, as his slave, floundering and resentful. I felt there was a lack of consistency in his expectations. There were times when his words lacked follow-through, and I often felt alone or like I wasn't serving well enough, but I didn't understand why, or how to make it better.

In hindsight, I believe I was experiencing a non-negotiated—and therefore not consented to—form of punishment. My impression was that he couldn't be bothered, or that he didn't want me, in those times. I understand now that deliberate action, follow-through and consistency are important, and that without these things, my boi would be on shaky ground. My being consistent with my words and actions gives my boi that solid foundation on which to stand.

*Speaking to my boi, I found they had been through similar experiences and had further feelings on the subject:*

*The bond between a slave and their Master is probably the most important one in a slave's life. They are unlikely to look to another person as they do to their Master due to the nature of the dynamic they share with their Master. That makes it even more hurtful when such a centre of one's universe chooses to cut them out in disappointment or disapproval.*

> Breaking through disappointment that's been expressed in a careless way can and will happen. It can also have lasting consequences that may have the exact opposite effect one intends, leading to even worse or more erratic behaviour in the submissive who has been broken down.

> Can an M-type express disappointment to their submissive for something said or done in daily life? Of course they can! They should. They're human just like everyone else. Should an M-type perhaps be mindful of the ways they express said disappointment? Definitely.

> If it goes wrong, are there ways to fix it? Of course! As long as a real instance of abandonment doesn't immediately happen thereafter to compound someone who's already feeling fragile, almost anything can be fixed with some time, dedication and affection. Dedication isn't only a thing that can be offered by a submissive. I feel like dedication to a dynamic comes ideally from both people in it.

As an older-generation cisgender man (he was 35 years my senior), my Master and I had very different communication styles and experiences. When he chose not to share what was bothering him, I didn't feel it was my place to pry into my Master's business. This often left us in very different spaces, and in the long term, it began to create a vast chasm between us.

Sometimes these communication differences would also lead to my Master just doing things himself instead of taking advantage of my service. To me, it seemed that he simply preferred to do things himself. It was his choice, for instance, if he wanted to take care of all the finances, rather than to teach his slave to help him.

This, however, turned out to be a double-edged sword. I ended up complacent in believing and trusting he had everything under control, but I also never really checked up on what things truly looked like. This taught me that although I can trust another person with financial control, it is also important to verify exactly how they are handling my finances to ensure that basic like bills get paid.

After he passed, I was in a situation where I had to relearn financial skills during what was one of the hardest emotional upheavals of my life. My boi also had a similar experience of relearning after the sudden end of one of their power exchange relationships:

*At the start, I found it incredibly difficult to do anything without first gaining permission. I had trouble with orgasming, because I'd had to ask permission to do so. Ditto with going to the toilet. Eating and drinking felt odd to do without asking, "Sir, may I please" at the table with whoever I was sitting with.*

*I started by deliberately walking out of the walking protocol I'd had, on the "wrong" side of people whenever I was out, so that I didn't fall back into habits of walking just behind the shoulders of friends. We build these dynamics up over months, over years, putting a great deal of thought into the things that make us hot, the things that bind us together more closely, the way that dynamics feel as they deepen.*

*But what happens when these relationships end suddenly? I know many people suggest a slave be passed to other, trusted, M-types in the case of a Master's demise. But what about the end of a dynamic where the Master chooses to walk away?*

*I feel as though at least as much thought needs to be put into how to safely separate a submissive or slave from their Master as is put into the excitement of building up a dynamic. Ideally, this could be thought about and agreed to ahead of time, with a Master having the integrity to hold to promises made in the start of a dynamic at the end of one.*

I answered from my experience. My Master understood there was every chance, given the age gap between us, that he would pass first, and so he made sure that he put people in place for when that time came—people who would understand the depth of my needs and mindset as a slave in the immediate aftermath. After he passed, both of those people came to me individually. Each of them used almost the exact wording, telling me they didn't know if I remembered the conversation we'd had, but that they each did and they were there to honour their word. Even now, years later, I call one of those people my god-Dom because he was there, he remained there, he was there for me, he's family. He stood for everything that family should be.

Should this current dynamic and relationship between my boi and I end, I would hope there would be someone as kind and dedicated that I could entrust them to if I were to pass. And as for us choosing to part ways, we have spoken of me slowly weaning them from the dynamic before that should ever happen.

Now I understand exactly how important it is to communicate, and this has ensured that my boi and I check in regularly with one another. We negotiated into our dynamic the ability to call "veranda time" as needed—veranda time being a time of equal sitting, where the power exchange between us is suspended for a specific period of time, and where each of us are able to speak freely about issues and concerns. In practice, it has offered the two of us the opportunity for ongoing negotiation of our dynamic without fear of repercussions.

My boi and I are both aware that matters of money still stress me out. When it comes to the almighty dollar, I become a grumpy wolf with a thorn in my paw. My boi, therefore, takes care of the finances in service to me, but they are also to keep an up-to-date spreadsheet of all our comings and goings. They should always, on request, be able to show me accounts and/or send me screenshots.

We have a transaction account that I control in order to help me to become less stressed with money, and to make sure I don't slip into old habits of not having control where it comes to finances. This is because we also agree that, just because one is on the M-side of the slash, that does not mean that they already know everything. I am in constant pursuit of self-growth, and my boi follows that example.

One lesson I am currently learning is how my protectiveness towards my boi sometimes leaves me stifling my own control and allowing them to, by proxy, top from the bottom. This comes from the fact that I don't wish to push them beyond their limits, to the point of causing emotional upheaval and meltdowns. But it comes with the downside that I often veer too much in the other direction. I sometimes forget that, by the very nature of our dynamic, we have both agreed that I have the ability to give instruction and to have that instruction followed. Not only has this been consented to by my boi, but as someone with a slave heart, my giving them instructions makes them happy and keeps them settled because they understand what is expected of them and their place at my feet is reinforced. In the few cases I've not given an instruction, then sulked about not having control, I've realised only belatedly that I've taken power away from myself in not using the communication skills already mentioned.

I experienced this over-protectiveness in my time as a slave, to my detriment. My Master would not allow me to do many of the forms of service that brought me joy because I had fibromyalgia, and he was fiercely protective about my health. But that protectiveness also took away my ability to serve, leaving me feeling like a broken and useless slave. These are feelings I never want to bring upon my boi if I can help it. This over-protective nature only sets them up to fail and that's the last thing I desire to do to them.

Finally, I know what it is to be set up to fail, or for it to at least feel that way. I had a dominant for a short period of time after my long-term Master passed. This dominant didn't quite seem to grasp the fact that I was still grieving; they expected that I would function exactly as they expected me to, that I would serve exactly as they had seen me serve him. Whether they meant it to or not, their expectations blinded them to other realities and, in turn, set me up for failure. I stayed on, despite my late Master's voice telling me, "Raising your hands in anger is abuse." No Master should raise their hands in anger. In my belief, consent can never be given in this instance because, when they are that angry, a person is not in control of themselves. Therefore, they can't be in control of another, or their consent.

I feel as though this dominant forgot I was a human being first and foremost. This part of my journey taught me some of the hardest lessons I have learned. One lesson it truly embedded in my mind for this current part of my journey, as Alpha to my boy, is that as well as being someone with a slave heart, they are also a human being with human frailties, emotions, needs. I remember this part of them is first, foremost and always. They are not a robot, and nor do I desire them to be.

---

*Alpha-Pup is a 39-year-old transman who identifies as an Alpha Slave, Daddy and Wolfdog. Alpha-Pup is the Owner, Alpha and Daddy of Boi-Nik, a 37-year-old multigendered slave, little, and handler of Alpha's dog self, Shadow.*

# Transitioning From Egalitarian To M/s
*Master Jim*

There are many ways to find oneself a member of what we collectively and loosely call the "lifestyle." Some of us enter into the realm of M/s not through a solo path of exploration and discovery, but rather as part of a couple transitioning from a pre-existing egalitarian relationship. I myself am in this latter category, having started my journey into power exchange from an established relationship. My slave and I have carefully transitioned our nearly thirty-year marriage into a thriving, successful Master/slave power exchange.

For clarity, I want to say at the outset that in this essay I will be sharing my personal journey and therefore will use the terms Master and slave, as these are the terms I apply to my own dynamic. Similarly, I refer to genders as they exist in my dynamic. While reading this, please substitute your own genders and preferred terminology for M-type and s-type roles. Additionally, it is imperative to state that no two dynamics are the same, and there are a myriad of unique and valid approaches to power exchange. Therefore, please take what you find useful, and most importantly make your path and dynamic your own.

## Beginnings

Our transition took place over many years and has had many phases. There are seeds of power exchange that go back pretty much to our beginnings. These seeds had to be nurtured and understood to reach their full potential, and along the way much insight was gained about the pitfalls and triumphs of cultivating an M/s dynamic from a longstanding egalitarian relationship. In this writing, I would like to share a little of the wisdom I have gained along the way with a specific focus on the perspective of the Master's path. I will recount things I learned on my journey by sharing details and thoughts on only a couple of the many aspects of our transition, since this essay simply cannot contain them all. M/s dynamics are complex and ever-evolving, continually facing new challenges. To this day our dynamic is a work in progress, as it always will be.

*In the beginning there was kink, and kink was good, and smiles were upon the faces of the couple.*

As many will attest, a common place to start one's journey into the world of power exchange is in the bedroom. It is, in fact, a good way for partners just starting out to "test the waters" of power exchange without straying too far down a path where all parties involved might not feel comfortable heading. Initially bounding the power exchange to the bedroom can help to foster a feeling of safety that allows for experimentation and growth within the safe space that has been created.

This was true for myself and my slave. In the beginning, before my wife also became my slave, we found the wonderful world of kinky sex. Like a breath of fresh air, it revitalized our relationship, making us feel giddy with excitement as we surfed the world of physical pleasures infused by a burgeoning power dynamic. What I learned during this period was that in order to have my sexual needs fulfilled, I could take charge and "good things" would happen. My willing partner responded eagerly to my dominance in the bedroom and later remarked that she was, above all, relieved that she no longer felt pressure to initiate or direct our intimate encounters. The point to emphasize here is that decision-making, even when it comes to such things as leisure and recreation, is still decision-making.

The early days of transitioning an egalitarian relationship is very much about feeling out where exactly each person comfortably sits relative to the other in terms of the developing power exchange. This needs to be done before venturing further than casual kink-fuckery. To this end, establishing frequent, clear, open, honest communication is one of the most important things a Master can do early in the process of transition. There are many discussions to be had, and doing so will take time and effort. This can be seen by the Master as another valuable opportunity to exercise leadership. My slave and I had countless meaningful and intense conversations. This allowed us to establish ourselves comfortably in our relative roles, discuss our feelings towards power exchange, and start to hammer out what we wanted from our unique dynamic. Taking responsibility in this way, as we explored our early kinky cravings, helped me determine that I definitely belonged on the left side of the slash, and allowed me to see the comfort my slave felt being on the right side. Further, it helped us realize we eventually did want to bring the power exchange "outside the bedroom." The power exchange we established for our kinky lives desired a broader outlet.

### Transition Beyond the Bedroom

The skills a Master acquires learning to lead in the bedroom can be transferred to leadership in day-to-day activities. Establishing roles, developing vision, exerting control—these are the bread and butter of ultimately taking the power exchange into more realms of one's existence. After my slave and I realized we were both interested in exploring the idea of having a 24/7 dynamic, I took steps towards making power exchange a more integral part of our everyday life. Though we both wanted this, time and time again we encountered difficulties and roadblocks to our forward momentum.

As a cautionary note, one should not travel far into the world of power exchange, either in the context of play or in a dynamic outside the bedroom, without first studying the collective wisdom concerning such topics as consent, safety, and clear communication, as well as a myriad of other "best practices". Here again is an opportunity for the would-be Master to start to practice leadership skills and exercise the vision and wisdom that will make him worthy of owning and accepting responsibility for his partner-turned-slave in an evolving power exchange. Though it falls on all parties to exercise responsibility, it is incumbent on the role of the Master to provide leadership.

When transitioning from an existing relationship, it is very possible that both people will be inexperienced and unfamiliar with the wider world of kink and power exchange. In our case, while we were well aware of the existence of this world, we had never sought to find it and engage more actively. We would not do so until far along into our power exchange journey. I learned early on that the best way to lead my slave forward in the direction we both espoused wanting to go was slowly, one gentle step at a time. It took a long time for my slave to feel comfortable exploring our interests out in the world, outside our safe little lives at home. One of the things I'm most proud of in our journey was that I did not push this point until she was comfortable venturing forth.

We approached this insular time as an opportunity to rediscover one another, as well as a period of self-discovery. During this time, we both sought to learn as much as we could about the broader elements of power exchange that we each found thrilling and invigorating. As a result of our inexperience and our temporary decision not to have contact with the wider community, we did experience some feelings of isolation as well as confusion and frustration. Though there is much that can be researched regarding power exchange, it can be daunting and often impossible to have the proper context to absorb and process the information one finds. Additionally, with so much information and advice to be found on the internet by newcomers to the lifestyle, it is difficult to discern the quality content from dubious information.

While I was learning the skills of leadership, during the many conversations we had in this period, I spent a great deal of time listening to my slave as I developed and shared my vision for our dynamic. At this time, I was leading and she was following. We were not yet in a 24/7 dynamic, though we were heading in that direction steadily, albeit slowly, and so our transition progressed without much angst. This is a good point to state that the elements of power exchange can exist and enrich one's life at many different levels of engagement. We were enjoying ourselves, and there is nothing wrong with that. While we talked a lot about how our future might look, we were not yet approaching fundamental changes to our relationship.

When the time came that my slave was more comfortable and felt safe to do so, I led us into the broader community. In hindsight, I consider this to be an example of me living up to my leadership responsibilities as a Master. I took my slave's needs into consideration and led her forward in a way that allowed her to fully embrace personal growth, and by extension fostered the growth of our dynamic. We started to attend events, and ultimately that led to meaningful interactions and many more educational and growth opportunities within a community of support.

### Facing the Larger Challenges of Transition

One of the significant differences between transitioning an existing egalitarian relationship into a power exchange dynamic, as compared to establishing a power exchange dynamic at the beginning of a relationship, is the existence of years of history and familiarity. Sometimes I feel wistful for the "purity" that I imagine might have existed if our relationship had originated as a power exchange from the outset—the opportunity to create something new without all the history of what "once was" impacting decision-making. The challenge for the Master is to provide the vision and the leadership to *transform* instead of to *establish*. In a new relationship, many elements such as protocols and rules can be decided ahead by the Master and only introduced into the dynamic as they serve the designs of the Master and the dynamic. The Master in a transitioning relationship, however, generally has better success by reshaping existing behaviors into protocols and instilling them with new meaning.

My best advice is to be clear, concise and tactical in exercising the new overarching vision. Transformation of a relationship is a large and often emotional project. I believe a fruitful way to move forward is to apply vision and focus on one area at a time. Trying to take on too much change at once can lead to stress for both the Master and the slave. A good place to initially focus is in areas where one has already noticed success—build on those and branch out. It won't always go according to plan, and the Master needs to be flexible and patient. I won't say that I got this perfectly right myself. As we brought our power exchange out of the bedroom and into our daily lives, there were many points at which I felt stymied and frustrated by the areas of the pre-existing relationship which were not yet transformed, or where we were finding friction.

### Familiarity: The Challenges

This brings us to another aspect of our transition that I want to explore. Familiarity can be a significant issue for transitioning a pre-existing relationship into a power dynamic. Depending on the relationship, there may be years or even decades of shared experience between the people involved, which has invariably created a lot of familiarity. My slave and I navigated our lives together for many years prior to transitioning our relationship. Over the course of those years we had experienced conflict regarding many different issues. Now that we were establishing a power exchange, those issues each would need to be revisited in the context of our growing dynamic. Disagreements that we'd had ten times over now had to be resolved differently. We knew this to be true, but it took time and patience for the truth of this to be lived out, for the behaviors actually to change into new patterns.

Familiarity such as we were experiencing can be quite troublesome because it can undermine the Master's ability to establish structure, which is an important element of many power exchange dynamics. Through structure, vision can be achieved. Additionally, structure provides the pathways through which power exchange can be experienced and enjoyed by the individuals in the dynamic.

However, creating the structure we both wanted in that atmosphere of familiarity was a recurrent impediment to my Mastery. One concrete example occurred as I tried to implement protocols of communication. Our discussions in the past had always been free-wheeling and occasionally devolved into arguments, sometimes heated. As we transitioned, our discussions became a challenge for me as they were rich with familiarity in the form of our old patterns of speech and behavior. Speech and behavior protocols are a common endeavour in many M/s dynamics, as they are purposeful ways to create structures designed to minimize conflict and foster clear communication. In our case, I found these protocols were hard to establish in the face of ingrained communication habits. I persevered, however, and found that, though challenging, carefully creating structure helped tame many of the negative patterns of interaction, while giving me an opportunity to reinforce new and existing desired patterns of communication.

It is important to realize that there is no one size fits all model for how one should go about developing structure. As I progressed in my journey towards Mastery, I was looking for the tools and techniques to establish structure in the face of the familiarity present in our relationship. I attended classes taught by others who had undergone similar transformations and faced the same challenge with familiarity, seeking an approach that I might utilize. In one class, the Master described how he had chosen to entirely set aside the personal aspects of their long-term existing relationship with all of its familiarity. He did this for a period of time until he believed the structure of the power exchange had been fully established in the "new" dynamic unfettered by the patterns of behavior that had been inherent in the preexisting relationship. At the time, this seemed to be a good way to overcome the difficulties of familiarity. This method had worked for the M/s couple leading the class, and it may be a successful path for others as well.

I found, however, when I tried to apply the elements of this approach to my own dynamic, the resulting effects were not at all what I expected. Instead of helping to fix our difficulties, I discovered that my slave had a strong negative reaction. My intent initially seemed simple: to establish structure absent interference from the past. For my slave, however, the mere thought of setting aside our existing deep emotional intimacy, even if for a worthy cause, took her to a place of feeling disconnected and abandoned.

Many tense moments came out of my efforts to determine what vision I would ultimately pursue for balancing our prior relationship with our growing power dynamic and how I would lead us towards this vision. This was perhaps the single most difficult challenge in our transition. I grappled with determining whether we should embrace the idea of two different relationships, as espoused by some in our community, or whether these two parts of our relationship, what we came to call our marriage and our dynamic, were related in ways that could not be disentangled. How could I best achieve the goals I had for creating structure given the knowledge I was building, and the challenges I was facing?

### Familiarity: The Blessings

Ultimately I decided that I needed to address the issue of familiarity not by setting aside our history, but by embracing and harnessing the positive aspects of the powerful bond we already had. I did this while keeping a watchful eye on patterns that needed redress when encountered—the skillful Master uses all the tools at his disposal. There is tremendous value in the trust, comfort and knowledge of one's partner. And through this process I came to understand that the bond of the familiarity my slave and I shared was a core component of my slave's calling to slavery. We had a beautiful history too, and I needed to remember that.

I came to realize fully that not all familiarity is negative, and one tool I could easily use was embracing the familiar moments that fed our dynamic. One small example of this: At the end of the day my slave and I like to settle down on the couch, snuggle, and watch television. This is a familiar comfortable activity carried forward from our earlier days, and this time in our day is imbued with great comfort and connection. Though from the outside this activity appears mostly the same today as it always was, within the context of our M/s relationship it has taken on a new meaning with subtle new protocols. We still settle down together on the couch, but before she settles in, my slave carefully removes my shoes and positions the ottoman so that I can stretch out comfortably as we enjoy a television program or two. The physical closeness often leads to moments of feeling intense dynamic connection, a connection that is amplified by the familiar activity now given new context. As bedtime approaches for my slave, who retires before myself, she whispers the following affirmation in my ear: "Thank you for owning me." To which I reply, whispering back into her ear: "Thank you for being mine." We have created a meaningful M/s ritual from the positive history of this simple activity.

### The Ongoing Path of Transition

I learned an important lesson in the context of leading throughout this process of transition: as Masters, we don't always have all the answers, and we must adapt to the facts as we discover them in our dynamics. I also cannot overstate the importance a community can have in helping to discover one's path to Mastery. Though I took many steps on my own, I am so much the richer for the many meaningful interactions and treasured insights I've had by engaging with my peers.

In the time since the initial years of transitioning our relationship, I have come to appreciate that there are some aspects to one's M/s dynamic that come naturally, and others which are much more demanding. From the moment we decided to embrace our kinky desires, our growth and movement towards developing our kinky side was comfortable for us—kinky power exchange came easily. Although we have had a few demanding moments here as well, we have always found that the physical side of our relationship is fundamental to the way we live out our M/s. Our most difficult hurdles fell primarily in establishing and managing our dynamic structure outside the bedroom. This was true even though we have always had an innate foundation of power exchange, which had evolved during our egalitarian marriage. As a Master, I learned to discern what came easily and naturally from the challenges that would require my closer attention and concerted efforts of leadership.

A common mistake of many Masters, myself included, is focusing too much on solving the hard problems and forgetting the successes one has already had. Drawing a lesson from this, as a Master I have found that it is important to make note of these successes because they are now important elements of one's dynamic, elements which one can turn to and fall back on when things get messy or tough. Managing an M/s relationship will surely test every Master at some point. I was tested as I tried to navigate and lead through the issues of creating structure in the face of familiarity. At these points, we need to be able to ground ourselves and move on, to manage the problems at hand, be they transient and tactical or more longstanding and fundamental. We need to celebrate the successes we have had and cherish the opportunities to grow in our dynamics over time. As Masters, we must lead according to principle and integrity, but also with compassion and caring, never losing sight of the human on the other side of the power exchange, and their needs, inherent value, and dignity.

Transitioning an egalitarian relationship to a thriving M/s dynamic is not just possible, it can be greatly rewarding and lead to a much closer, healthier and harmonious existence for the individuals involved. That said, it is not without risk. At some point during the transitioning of our relationship, we both realized that we had changed in ways that would be impossible to undo. We had reached the point of no return, and we could no longer retreat to the perceived "safety" of our previous egalitarian marriage. Transition itself had become transformational to us as individuals. We were no longer the same people, and there was no going back. While all this was true, neither had we left our marriage behind; it too remained a fundamental part of our relationship. We now have our marriage with all of its familiarity intertwined with our M/s dynamic with all of its support structures. We continue to reconcile these two interwoven but distinct aspects of our relationship. As a Master, I continue to provide the leadership, vision and structure needed to experience and strengthen our dynamic. This is the ongoing work of a transitioning relationship.

A smile is still on my face ... and my slave is smiling too.

# Polyamory and the Territorial M-type

*Raven Kaldera*

When people combine the alternative relationship practices of polyamory and power dynamics, it creates even more areas of relationship negotiation where one can't just lean back and assume, but must then figure out how to do this thing in a way that is custom-built for the couple involved. In this case, the issue is what to do when the subordinate partner in a consenting power dynamic wants to have outside partners, and the dominant partner finds that the idea threatens their feeling of dominance in the relationship.

Some people who read this will just shrug and say snippily, "Well, too bad, that means they're just insecure and they should just get over it." This attitude is neither useful, kind, effective, nor necessarily true. It also shows, in some cases, a lack of understanding about the emotional side of being the dominant party in a relationship, especially one with a high level of authority transfer.

Every person who takes on this role is going to have a different subjective scale in their head which indicates what needs to happen for them to feel like the role is actually meaningful and not some pretend thing cooked up as a fun role-play. That scale can't just be altered at will to make the s-type more comfortable, because it's about emotions. In the end, a potential D-type or M-type can make all the noble rules they want, but if they don't take their subjective meaningful-role scale into account, they will be constantly vaguely unsatisfied, and no amount of sexy prancing about by the s-type is going to alleviate that. At worst, it will cause a seeping resentment that will eventually poison the dynamic, often appearing as the dominant partner slowly losing interest in doing their agreed-upon "acts of dominance" and letting things slip sullenly back into an egalitarian situation.

This scale is irrational, and it must be satisfied in some way or the job will feel meaningless. It may also have gradations—for example, with myself, what I need to feel like a limited D/s relationship with a submissive partner is real and meaningful is different from what I would need out of a relationship with someone who calls themselves my slave and property.

When these power dynamics are negotiated, they usually start out slowly and with only a few areas of authority transfer (which I believe is how it should be), and new areas may or may not be added over time. Sometimes the transfer of authority proceeds in a way where the D-type or M-type gets enough new areas of responsibility that they find themselves pushed up to a new level of authority without getting enough of that scale checked off to feel like they are getting enough of the juicy parts back. ("You want me to take responsibility over all these things, and you won't give me *that?*")

Also, sometimes a D-type or M-type can say with complete honest intention, "Your freedom and agency in that area won't bother me at all," and they absolutely mean it, and then it actually happens, and they are surprised and possibly shocked by the strength of their unexpected feelings on the matter. We're all flawed human beings and we've all been there—you don't know that you want something until you don't have it anymore. It happens. It would be nice if declaring one's self a master automatically made one into a saintly being capable of constant unconditional love, but it doesn't work that way.

So let's say that for whatever reason the dominant partner said yes to polyamory (of some sort) for both people in the negotiations, and at some point realized that the s-type's poly plans were making them feel like their role was being undermined. (If the two parties didn't actually negotiate beforehand how the polyamory would work, that's a different problem, and it's back to the drawing board for both people.) I'm going to suggest a three-step plan with tips and tricks to help them with their evolution around the issue, one that lays no blame and casts no shame and might actually be useful.

### Step 1: Check Motivation

I've often said that there are four big demons of polyamory. I use my own terms to define them, terms that in general language are pretty vague, but I've redefined them for specificity. If you don't like my terms and their definitions, please substitute your own while reading. The D-type or M-type should do an honest (and perhaps painful) self-evaluation of what combination of demons they are harboring.

❖ *Jealousy* is insecurity in one's worth ("You'll find someone better than me and leave me for them") or in one's position ("I can't trust you to stick with me in the haze of new relationship energy with someone else"). If this is one of the problems, have your partner (or a therapist) work with you on self-esteem so that you'll feel more worthy, or work with the partner on finding reasonable and practical ways they can build your trust in them.

❖ *Possessiveness* is scarcity consciousness. ("There won't be enough of your presence/time/energy/love to go around if I share you! I won't get enough!") For this, lay out the potential problems and set up some rules around how these possibly scarce resources can be distributed. Make sure to include an honest definition of "enough", perhaps outlining what the selfish/scared part of your wants, what will definitely be unacceptable, and what happy medium would be perhaps not perfect but acceptable.

❖ *Territoriality* is a tough one. It's generally only found in people whose personality is very "alpha", although sometimes it can develop in others when they are put in certain situations. It's less of a merely emotional problem and is more of a lizard-brain issue—it harks back to a more primitive "animal" time when one defended one's territory because it was one's food survival, and if that part of your brain has decided that this s-type is your "territory", encroachment can cause a feeling of survival-panic. If someone has this, the more dominant they are expected to be in the relationship, the worse it gets, in my experience. It takes a lot of mental jiggering to work against it. For this problem, see the last section on "Reframing".

❖ *Envy* is another tough one. That's when your partner has a partner and you don't, and you're resentful and want them to wait until you have someone and don't have to be sitting alone. Different people have different "market value" out there, and it's never a fair distribution. For this one, my advice is to keep hoping, keep praying, and in the meantime, spend that time working on yourself to build yourself into a more awesome human being. Learn new skills and get good at them. Develop your talents. Work on your personality. Get out there in groups and meet people. In real time.

### Step 2: Check Levels

Spend some time learning about and writing down different levels of power exchange. It doesn't matter what names or labels you use. If the varying definitions for what seems like every single word used in public forums bothers you, just describe them. Do an honest self-inventory of what you need to feel like you're actually in charge at each level. For example, if you were a manager at work, would you feel the title was meaningful if you couldn't fire anyone, couldn't level any consequence for bad behavior, couldn't hire anyone new, and could only speak to each employee for five minutes per week? Consider what is important to your irrational subjective feelings about a meaningful role at different extremities of power exchange. Then bring this to the s-type, and ask them to write down a similar list—what makes them feel like their role is real at each level? It's worth comparing lists, and it can help you both figure out where you are, and where you want to be in the future (which doesn't have to change, but it's good to know if one party is hoping for more and the other one isn't).

Also, look at levels of polyamory. Where do your issues kick in? That anyone touches them sexually at all? Is an egalitarian partner OK, but not another dominant one? What about a submissive one? Is a vanilla partner OK, but not a kinky one who would want to do BDSM? Or is it falling in love and becoming attached that would bother you? This, too, should be discussed with the s-type. It maybe that they aren't even thinking about what you fear most.

### Step 3: Reframing

Many situations can be reframed to feel more acceptable to one's inner scale. The s-type can be a big help with this, if they know what you're going for. Rules and protocols can be put in around situations— how do we refer to this sort of thing in a way that reinforces who we are together? See if any of these help you.

1) S-type wants another partner? The two of you could go looking together, as a team. That's best with poly anyway. If you two approach other people together, so you can be assured that it's someone you respect and work well with, someone you get along with, not some stranger that you're imagining all sorts of bad things about. If you have some control in the choice process, that can help assuage the feelings of losing control over them.

2) Can you think of the s-type as your "thing" which you are lending out to someone else because you are a generous monarch giving largesse to his people? That you are so sure about your hold on them that you don't mind giving them as a gift? That thought-twist brought me through some rough times. Of course, you do actually have to be secure enough about the relationship to trust them. (See the "jealousy" issue.)

3) Can it be made clear that you have priority, perhaps get to set a few rules about what the other partner can do and not do? Or that there are special things you can do with them to "reclaim" them and "mark your territory" after they have time with the other partner? That helped me a fair amount. Just make sure that your "reclaiming" is fun for both parties, and is tinged with confidence, not anger and insecurity.

4) Is the putative other partner going to know about the power exchange? Can you insist that they understand it and are OK with it? (Let me tell you how weird and awkward it gets when they aren't comfortable with it! That isn't just about personal insecurity, it's about heading off future trouble later.) Can they be asked to help in little ways—being able to say, "Thank you so much for lending me your thing! He/she is wonderful and I'm fortunate that you are willing to share." Someone who understands power exchange might be willing to work with this. Someone who doesn't will likely find it discomfiting, along with most of the rest of what you do. But if it can happen, at least in the beginning until you're used to them/the relationship with them, every bit of positive reinforcement helps.

5) If you can find a way to cope and be OK with the s-type doing this, you've got a leg up on other D-types who probably won't. It will be obvious that you're the good partner, the one who is willing to make

compromises in order to make sure her needs are met. Keep this in mind as a benefit. One of the mantras that helped me is, "I'm the one who has, and I can afford to be generous."

And, finally, a last sobering reality: Power dynamic relationships require more initial compatibility than egalitarian ones, and the more extreme the authority transfer, the more initial compatibility is required. This is because the more places you're automatically on the same page, the less the s-type has to sacrifice. If you don't have the initial compatibility to do this, or do it at more than a limited level, that is no one's fault. It's just life. It's possible that this won't work— that the dominant partner's internal "scale" is just so far away from the desires and preferences of the s-type that there's no bringing it together. If that's the case, you both have hard decisions to make. Try not to make them with blame, but with honest nonjudgmental sorrow and understanding.

# Mentorship
*Mistress Sky*

Mentorship is a short-term trusting relationship with a respected and very experienced master which is created for the new learner's enrichment. New dominants in power exchange relationships can learn from reading books and articles and from attending educational events about power exchange, but in addition, there is so much that is very special about meeting with a mentor, a real person who wishes only the best for you and yours.

A new dominant may have a vast number of questions that so far have gone unanswered, and will benefit from having someone of whom they can ask questions. Mentoring is a social process that is intended to benefit the mentee. A mentor can be defined as a type of *life guide*, a knowledgeable person who is farther down the road than you in some specific area. They can be an anchor in the sweet stream of crazy new experiences in the world of kink. The mentor's advice can be invaluable for staying safe within our kink communities, and spending time with one might help you to figure out how to incorporate safety into your unequal relationship.

Mentors should be both honorable and humble, remembering that this is giving service, a contribution to our community. It's all about the mentee's needs. It's the mentee's life that we hope to aid, and our satisfaction is derived by assisting another to move further along their journey. Leaving the mentees better off is our only payment. The idea of more experienced people helping those who are just beginning their kink path is an old and highly respected tradition.

Mentors are *not* play partners, counselors, coaches, trainers or parent figures. Mentoring refers to giving guidance, but it does not quite cross into teaching—the mentor is not a tutor. Giving recommendations or suggesting resources is distinctly different from coaching. Offering encouragement is not the same as training. A mentor should be able to share life experiences with a mentee as a guiding hand without becoming a parent telling the mentee what he should or should not do.

The mentorship commitment is short term and clearly defined within a narrow area of learning for the mentee. A specific time is declared and agreed on. Mentors should be models of high integrity and appropriate behavior, as well as being a model for the specialty that the mentee wants to grow in. Even though someone might serve in more than one role for you—such as teacher *and* mentor—that person should be very good at keeping the roles separate and not blurring the lines. This effort is part of the mentor's integrity.

## Who Can Be a Mentor?

❖ Dominants mentor other dominants.
❖ S-types mentor other S-types.

There are a few formal programs offered by organizations, led by a well-known individual of long experience, but these are currently rare. Mostly, mentorship is a private matter between two individuals who agree to spend time together for a little while.

## Upon Being Approached, How Does a Mentor Behave?

Those of us who think that we know something worth sharing *do not solicit mentees.* Someone might approach us and ask if we might be open to the idea of mentoring them. We might agree to have a conversation, but nothing more can be promised because we have just met them. We might also say "No, sorry, I don't have any extra time. However, if you have questions about a particular power exchange topic right now, I wouldn't mind talking about my experiences while I'm still here at the club." In other words, if you approached one of us and asked about being mentored, we would not just say "Yes!" and the relationship is launched. That scenario is pure fantasy.

When someone approaches me for mentoring, these are some of my immediate thoughts. This will give you an idea of what to expect. Use this information to govern your own behavior.

❖ What's my first impression of this person? How do I feel?
❖ What is the person's main interest? Am *I* interested in what they are talking about?
❖ What's interesting about this person? What do I feel drawn toward—personality or topic or both?

>="3">

- How specific was the prospective mentee's request?
- How much have they invested in thinking through where the mentorship should be focused?
- Can I trust this person?
- Will I be proud of their choices and direction in life later?

I have to go away and think about this, including figuring out if I can spare some time for mentoring. I have to feel that this person is serious about self-development and not just likely to waste my time.

### How Do You Choose a Mentor?

You might be surprised to learn that it is a mutual decision to enter into mentorship. That is, you are to investigate whether this is the right person for you just as the prospective mentor has to evaluate whether they want a close association with you. Here are sets of questions to aid your thinking:

- Do they have a support network or operate as a loner?
- Do you see evidence of their good character?
- Are they good listeners?
- Are they emotionally erratic or calm and peaceful?
- Are they humble?
- Have you seen with your own eyes that they are respectful of others?
- How does the prospective mentor react if you don't appear open to their advice?
- What happens to the emotional tone of the conversation when you voice a different opinion than theirs?
- Are they pushy?
- Do they seem to have an agenda? Does mentoring seem to mean to them that you must follow their way of doing things?
- Do they seem to be looking for followers?
- Does this person present well at first but behave very differently when there is no crowd around? You are looking for evidence of their personal integrity.
- Does this person respond patiently, reasonably, and graciously, or is their ego at the surface?
- Do they appear to be committed to personal growth—theirs and that of others?

❖ Do they have references? It's okay to ask; they should ideally be well-known in their community. Other people should be able to say that the prospective mentor has been around for a long time and is known for their expertise in a particular area. You need to observe how they treat others, how are they regarded in the community, whether they are obviously contributing to community, whether others are asking for their opinion.

❖ As you spend a little time with this person, do you feel that their interest in you as a person, along with interest in your topics, is sincere and genuine?

❖ Later on, in your conversations with them, do they easily admit to mistakes if there are any? As such, they are modeling the same desirable behavior for you.

❖ If there is a problem within the community, do they abstain from spreading gossip?

❖ Do they encourage you and others toward positive actions that benefit everyone, or do they mindlessly contribute to confusion?

You and your prospective mentor might meet a couple of times before the mentor begins to suggest that the two of you might make a good pairing. If you agree, then the mentor should be very specific about what he or she is willing to offer. Mentors must consider how much time they can afford to give, as well as what content they are experienced with and are willing to discuss. The mentor might have specific assignments for you, or requests (within reason) such as attending certain events that would help you, or a reading list that they want you to cover in addition to your discussion meetings. Given that you should be considered a peer, you have the right to politely refuse assignments.

It's more than okay to make your own proposal for how mentorship will proceed. Maybe, you will listen to the mentor's proposal and then ask for a modification or two. You must go away and really think about your time and your willingness to dig deep, emotionally and otherwise, so that you get the most from mentorship. The more you put in, the more you will gain. Mentors usually only want to spend time with people who are serious about pursuing their own personal growth.

If after meeting with you once or twice the prospective mentor declares that the two of you are probably not the best match, then your response must be gracious and appreciative—no temper tantrums. You may ask if they have other suggestions for your learning path; maybe a different dominant would serve better as a mentor for you. Perhaps they do not have specific people recommendations in mind for you, but they feel certain that reading certain books would help you greatly. Thank the person for meeting with you.

### My List of Undesirable Traits in a Mentor

* Telling people only what they want to hear.
* Gossiping and attempting to draw you into negative talk.
* Narcissism or self-centered behavior.
* Jumping on the bandwagon.
* Attacking a weaker person in order to make themselves look good.
* Carrying a hidden agenda.
* Over-talking and dominating the conversation.
* Over-promising and under-delivering.
* Not being truthful.
* Objectifying others.
* Trying to isolate you by making rules about who you can socialize with.
* Holding court. He or she wants all eyes on him/her/them.

### What a Mentor Does Not Do

* A mentor does not dominate the mentee or expect to be served in any way. Mentees do not double as servants or submissives.
* A mentor does not bully the mentee or insist on doing things his/her particular way. Mentees are not clones of the mentor.
* A mentor will not suggest anything sexual. The mentor does not make inappropriate propositions.
* A mentor does not have play scenes with mentees.
* A mentor does not insist on knowing very personal information.
* A mentor does not solicit mentees for business or personal gain.
* Mentors will not ask you for money or payment-in-kind in exchange for their time.

But don't worry. *Your* mentor will never do any of those undesirable things.

### What Are a Mentor's Duties?

Your mentor should speak generally about the kink world and tell you many things, such as how to keep you and yours safe. This is all good social context for you, so take it in. Then, he or she should answer your power exchange questions to the best of his/her ability. The mentor might steer you to the right person to answer questions they cannot cover.

We might make suggestions to our mentees: "Try this, or look here." We can lead you toward resources, such as respected literature on power exchange, and sources for finding out about educational events.

Your mentor should be a kind and patient listener. They might act as your first "trust buddy" and agree to meet you at your first munch. They are steering you toward community, but not telling you with whom to be friends or loading you up with gossip. Your mentor should always aim to impart a deeper understanding of why we, dominants, do what we do, and encourage you to participate in community.

Mentors are not about the Doing—tasks, activities, learning how to flog. If you need lessons in flogging, ask one or more tops that you admire to spend time with you and train you. If you want conversations about flogging, or what it means to bottom or top, or how to negotiate play and give aftercare, then find a trainer. Instead, a mentor is your trusted source to bounce your own ideas off of. They are about the Why: the meaning and application of power exchange in our lives, dominance strategies, the submissive response to dominance with its countless variations, types of dominance or styles, bonding with your s-type, keeping your dynamic strong, maintaining excellent communication with your s-type, problem solving, negotiation, judging a good submissive match, figuring out what you most want from an unequal relationship, encouraging your submissive, or what true consent means. What can any of this power exchange stuff mean for your life and for your s-type? Ask all your questions! The mentor will look for opportunities to add a deeper understanding to the mentee's questioning on a subject.

### How Might a Mentor Help, and What Is Your Responsibility?

Keep in mind that mentorship is for you and is shaped by *your* interests. Tell the mentor what you are interested in discussing. Make an effort to be clear about what you wish to work on. If you agree to go forward with it, remember that the mentorship should have a narrow concentration. It's okay to only be prepared with a few single ideas. Maybe you have read repeatedly about negotiating with an unequal partner, but now you have many questions. Maybe your interest is purely your own unfamiliar feelings of dominance—what to do with all those feelings. You have plenty to mull over. You would do well to have a guiding hand as you are figuring out where you stand as a dominant/leading partner.

Expect to have lots and lots of internal dialogues from now on. How will you decide how your dominance is defined? What standards will guide your behavior toward your s-type? What do you want to gain from a real unequal partnership? What is reasonable to expect from your s-type? What might you help the s-type to gain from the relationship? Are you communicating well with your s-type? How do you judge good communication? Are you regularly checking in with your s-type or are you guessing at their reactions and how he/she/they feel? How do their various reactions make you feel? These and more are good questions to use the mentorship to explore. You will find your own balance, but it's good to have a mentor around as you are discovering your sense of self as a dominant. When you do, your main responsibility is to yourself—do the internal work that makes you the best dominant/leading partner/master that you can be, at every moment. The mentor expects to see that you are working hard.

Must you agree with absolutely everything that the mentor is saying? No. This is not expected. If the two of you are a good fit, most of the time you will find yourself in agreement with their perspective. It's not an accident that the two of you chose each other, but there are no absolutes—instead, you are expected to try on their wisdom like a coat of many colors. See how that last anecdote she told feels inside you. Think through the experiences that you shared with her by reassessing what happened through the analytic lens that she was able to offer you. You must come to your own conclusions, which you should voice to your mentor. With her guidance, you will find your own way—no more coat that you were just trying on, anyway. You will truly be a stronger and more able leader because you did the work to get there.

Remember, whatever amount of time that the mentor is able to give you is a gift, so you want to express gratitude. Always be respectful of the mentor's time. You can show respect by taking responsibility for scheduling meetings, by showing up on time, and by keeping to the agreed-upon time frame for your meetings. Mentorship can last a few days in a row or for the next four Fridays or for several sessions over one or two weekends. Mentorship could take place as monthly meetings for six months to a year.

### How to Find a Mentor

Munches. Meet-and-Greets. Events, private and public. Private parties. Recommendations from social friends. All of these and more are viable for your search. Respectfully approaching an experienced dominant online could net you an exploratory conversation or, at least, a lead or two. Spread the word widely that you are looking.

Community events that have a purpose of introducing prospective mentors and mentees are not frequently found, but they do happen. If there is no such thing in your local kink community, ask about it and offer to help to initiate one. Speak openly about mentorship as the phenomenal support that it can be for you and for others.

With the help of a good mentor, you can expect to become more on the mark of who you really are. You will have a lot to offer an unequal partner because you did the work to become the best master that you always knew you could be.

# Mastery and Risk Assessment
*Raven Kaldera*

Every day that I'm a Master, or at least every week, I roll the dice. I take a risk with my slave and our relationship, or I avoid one. The further you walk along this path, the more you realize that mastery is day-to-day risk assessment, which is why doing it well is one of the hardest things you'll ever do. (And ideally the most rewarding, but that depends on other factors.)

Power dynamic relationships are built on trust. That's not just the s-type's trust of the M-type acting with fairness and decency, although that's a huge issue. It's also the M-type's trust that the s-type will obey when given an order, that the M-type is able to make an impact on the world via their opposite number. In these relationships, acts that build trust are money in the bank, and acts that destroy trust are shooting yourself in the foot. Given this basic assumption, why would any M-type push their s-type beyond their comfort zone—or even to the edge of it—if this risks damaging their trust?

However, sometimes it's the right thing to do. The hard part is knowing when that is an option, and when it most definitely is not. In the early stages of a power dynamic relationship—and by this I mean at least the first two years—the M-type needs to listen to the s-type's information about themselves, their motivations, and their ability to change and adapt to new things. Decisions about whether to engage in high-risk activities should be based on the s-type's assessment of themselves. This is especially important for s-types whose self-assessment has been ignored or disrespected in the past, perhaps by parents or ex-lovers. Showing that you respect what they tell you about themselves will make them feel safer, and also promote further honesty, which you want. In fact, even if the M-type doesn't actually believe every word of that self-assessment, giving it at least basic respect and provisionally using it as a basis for decisions in the early phases is useful trust-building.

At the same time, the M-type needs to be closely watching the s-type to see how they function, especially in difficult situations. Don't deliberately create difficult situations in order to see that; Life always sends some over sooner or later anyway, so there's no need to do anything but wait. Watch for the circumstances when they push themselves, and when they indulge themselves. Watch for their fears and their moments of denial. Have discussions about these. This is something you should be doing anyway, because the more you can get into the s-type's head and understand how they tick (especially in the ways they are radically different from you as a person) the better decisions you will make about handling them.

However, a few years into the relationship, there may come a time when an M-type is really one hundred per cent certain that when the s-type says, "I can't do that," they are not stating a fact that is strictly true. They may believe it is true, but the M-type may feel that they could, indeed, do that thing, if the circumstances were correct. The hard part is being sure that's correct. M-types who push that too soon, or on an incorrect assumption, often lose their s-types. When you come to that point—believing that you know the s-type better than they know themselves—accept that you could be right, and you could be wrong. Examine your hopes and desires around the s-type being able to move in a particular direction. If those hopes and desires are strong, it is possible that your judgment is more affected by them than by the reality of the situation. Even if you are correct, those hopes and desires may make you push harder and faster than you should. Ideally, you should find a neutral third party with some perspective to talk to about it.

But if you never push the s-type to improve, or try something new and possibly scary, or face issues that are getting in the way of their happiness, growth in the relationship stalls out. Some people on either side of the slash may feel that growth is overrated, that they don't need any improvement, and that a nice quiet rut is the way to go. However, power dynamic relationships in general tend to bring up buried issues, so if it's going to happen anyway, you might as well use the power dynamic for self-improvement on both people's parts.

In addition, never pushing the s-type to do better out of fear of making them uncomfortable means that the s-type's emotions, and not the M-type's judgment, is in charge. There's also that s-types often internalize the M-type's view of them, and seeing them as unable to improve or too weak to push themselves can eventually cement their own view of themselves as incapable. On the other hand, the M-type believing in them and their ability to make progress can be immensely powerful, and if the s-type is never challenged, that power remains unused.

On the other side, if you do push your s-type, you run the risk that they might fail, and then you will be blamed for incorrectly assessing their abilities and setting them up for failure. If that happens, you can guarantee that trust will be damaged. But if they succeed, it will enhance their feeling of strength and competence. Success also means that they will be more likely to trust your judgment about their judgment even more, and trust will be expanded.

If you ask your s-type to do something difficult, and then back off when they are uncomfortable in order to be merciful, they may be grateful. They may also be angry because it means that you think they are weak, and you'll risk reinforcing a view of them as unable. They may feel both grateful and angry at the same time.

Do you see now why I'm saying that mastery is constant risk assessment? Of course it doesn't end there. Not all s-types will be a storm of conflicting emotions, but some will—especially if it's their first time, or their first time in a serious real-world authority transfer. It can be both thrilling and terrifying to be in that position, and on some days it's going to be less thrilling and more terrifying. If nothing else, they are forcing themselves to trust important parts of their life to someone whom they know will, eventually, let them down … if only because that person is a flawed and imperfect human being. It's important for the M-type to be patient and compassionate when they swing back and forth between two poles of fear and desire.

No one issue is relevant to every power dynamic, but there are a few that we've seen again and again, and one of them is the s-type who says, "I want you to push me to be better," and in fact may have sought out a power dynamic for the purpose of being pushed to improve in ways they couldn't manage themselves. Then, when the M-type takes them at their word and tries it, they freak out and push back with everything they have. Most decent M-types will just back off, bewildered. "But you said you wanted that! What happened?"

Let's do some translating here. When the s-type says, "I will do that," sometimes they mean, "I want to be able to do that." When they say, "I want that," sometimes they mean "I want to want that." When they say they want to be pushed, and then lash out when you do it, it's usually because they didn't realize it would feel as bad as it did. In these cases, the best thing to do is to acknowledge that—"Did that feel worse than you thought it would?"—and then back off a little (but not all the way) and discuss how it can be made easier. Moving to problem-solving in a calm manner can make it feel like an actionable setback, not a failure on their part.

It can be pretty demoralizing to the M-type, though. If the two of you have an intimate relationship, this might be a good time for the M-type to reveal how it feels on their end. "When you do that, I feel confused and I can't help wondering if you really want to be here in this relationship. If I keep pushing and I do real damage, I'll feel like an asshole. I don't want to be forced into being the bad guy, and I feel like the situation sets me up for failure. I'm not the enemy. We're on the same side, OK? Can we work together on this?" Sometimes the best way to snap an s-type out of their penduluming emotions is to show that you're a human being with feelings just like them, if you can manage to do it in a way that is connecting and not accusing.

Sometimes the risk assessment is around conflicting needs. The M-type needs to take four separate points into consideration when looking at the needs in a situation:

❖ The needs of the M-type.
❖ The needs of the s-type.
❖ The needs of the relationship itself.
❖ The needs of future sustainability.

Sometimes all four of those needs are going to clash, and unfortunately there is no automatic order of preference. It's a matter of considering each one carefully, in order to prioritize them. Look particularly for which one is most at risk. (One mistake of rookie M-types, when it comes to the first point on that list, is to be more comfortable pushing for desires that seem dominant, or "the sort of thing that masters want," while being less willing to stick up for their own more vulnerable and less stereotypically "masterful" hurt emotions.) If you have to vote against one of them, immediately work on figuring out how to balance that out. You may need to promise that the losing motivation gets prioritized up front the next time around.

I'll give you an example from our own lives. At some point a few years into the relationship, my slaveboy came to me and told me that he wanted a different career than the one for which he'd gone to school. It was too high-powered and rigid to focus on being my slave—which he felt was his first job—and he was learning that he hated corporate culture. He wanted something which would be more flexible, and which he would enjoy more … and if it gave me pleasure as well, that would be a huge bonus. After some consideration I settled on massage therapy. It had all those qualities, but the drawback was that he'd have to go back to school. Since I'd chosen it for him, it was up to me to send him, and to endure what would follow.

In order to make things work financially, he entered an intensive program as part of a degree in complementary health care which had him doing twenty-one credits at a time, plus an internship. He was almost never home, and when he was, he was exhausted. On my part, it was two years of having to give up his service most of the time, which made me very unhappy. I'd voted for the future, and I was sacrificing the other three items on the list for that. Of course, we talked about it regularly, and found small pieces of time to nourish our relationship. I told him that if he absolutely couldn't take the pace anymore, he could quit, but I knew his desire to make me proud would be stronger than his unhappiness at the situation. When I was angry or sad that he wasn't there to serve me, I reminded myself that this was short-term loss for long-term gain.

The situation was made even worse by the fact that some of his classmates—on whom he had to practice massage, and allow them to practice on him—were homophobic, so in order to avoid more conflict and tension he didn't talk about his relationship at all. I basically had to cease to exist in his life while he was at school, as far as socializing went. This made him avoid socializing on top of the rest of the stress.

As soon as he graduated, we treated ourselves to some months of intensive time together, feeding the first three items on the list. To cap it off, he got a tattoo on his arm that said "Raven's Boy", a promise to each other that we would never again closet our relationship. We don't regret that difficult period, because it got us long-term gain, but we could not have survived it without constant check-ins, finding places to fit in each other's needs, comforting each other when times got hard … and my constant belief that this was a worthy and achievable goal. My faith in my decision had to be the anchor that held our boat in the storm.

On the other hand, if I had realized that I'd miscalculated, I would have acknowledged that I was wrong, pulled up the anchor, pulled him out of school, and changed the plan. It's important to be humble and straightforward about when you make a mistake. Every s-type secretly wishes that this person who's making decisions for them was never wrong, and newer s-types can find it frightening during the first few periods of weathering the M-type's mistakes. It's important to remember that you need to form a track record … not of never erring, but of reacting maturely when you do make a mistake. That includes cleaning up the mess as best you can, and doing work to figure out how to avoid that particular pitfall in the future. Eventually, over time, an s-type can relax into serving a flawed human being who sometimes rolls the dice and loses, because they know that they won't ever be left alone with the consequences, and that the relationship can handle any amount of mopping up. That's real security—not believing that nothing bad can happen, but that when (not if) bad things happen, the two of you can get through it together every time.

# When the Slave is Above Your Pay Grade

*Raven Kaldera*

Finding an appropriate partner when you're just starting out as a would-be master or mistress is not easy. We've said before that these relationships need a higher initial level of compatibility than egalitarian ones, because the more values, ethics, goals, and expectations you share, the less the slave has to sacrifice for the master … and the less the master has to sacrifice for the relationship. However, since we're talking a very, very small niche of people, it's going to take a long time to find the right person. Keep the numbers game—and the very long odds—in your mind when you feel discouraged.

However, sometimes seekers on both sides of the slash decide that they are willing to settle for someone who isn't a good fit, but they want this dynamic badly enough that they try hard not to look at that. Sooner or later, of course, it goes awry and they break up—usually sooner. If the problem was just incompatibility, that's painful enough, but sometimes it's worse than that. We've all heard horror stories about would-be slaves who had terrible experiences with masters who looked sexy and dominant but were actually uncaring, narcissistic, violent, or any number of other harmful qualities. But what does the beginning master need to watch out for?

When my daughter was ten years old, we moved to the country, just down the road from a horse stable. She decided that she wanted a horse and my ex was willing to pay for it, so we went horse shopping in the classified ads. I knew nothing about horses and was completely at sea when it came to choosing them. Fortunately, the nice lady who ran the stable helped us to look through the ads and translate them. We saw the term "Needs experienced rider" fairly frequently. The stable-keeper said that phrase translated to "Has behavior problems." She followed that up with a firm statement about how that didn't mean it was a bad horse. On the contrary, the right person might be able to do wonders with that horse … but it was absolutely inappropriate for a beginning rider like my daughter.

The horse situation echoed in my mind as a metaphor when I saw new M/s relationships that foundered because the would-be slave had some serious problems—usually mental illness, addiction, or severe past trauma of some kind—that the dominant partner didn't have the experience and knowledge to handle. They'd both start out in good faith, hopeful that this would work out. Often the s-type was incredibly grateful that the M-type was willing to jump into the pool with them in spite of their problems; sometimes they hoped that the M-type would be able to "master" them out of their complications. Sometimes the M-type believed this illusion as well. And then there were the times when the s-type didn't tell the M-type about their issues, or didn't believe that they had any, or thought that they had them entirely under control.

Frequently, however, things got worse. The slave's behavior went out of control and the master didn't know what to do. Perhaps the master backed off, perhaps they clamped down and applied harsh punishments. Whatever they tried, it didn't work for one reason or another. The slave fell further down their black hole, perhaps blaming the master for not being able to stop it. Eventually it all fell apart. Some of those breakups were simply sad, some quite ugly.

The first problem was that the master was not an experienced enough rider for this particular horse. Dealing with a partner who has issues with mental illness, trauma, or addiction can be very difficult, especially if you're all alone with it. Trying to manage them and anything their disorder touches (which can end up being everything) requires a fair amount of specialized knowledge and skill that is not necessarily available to most people. It's throwing someone off the side of a boat into the ice-cold ocean when they've never learned to swim and have no life preserver. Good intentions, an urge to protect, even love—these things are not nearly enough.

Second, in some cases the slave hoped that their master would be able to fix them, or make them a safe space where they wouldn't have to deal with the world, or perhaps any responsibilities at all, including to the relationship. Countless new would-be masters have fallen into the trap of the white knight rescuer who thinks that they, armed with an idealistic view of M/s, can save the would-be slave. *Don't believe it.*

*Don't buy the story. It doesn't work.* Masters can't fix slaves. In some cases they've been able to create a supportive space for the slave to take on the work of fixing themselves, with help from outside professionals, but that's not the same thing. (In some cases, a good M-type can help if the only serious problem is that the s-type is making bad life choices due to circumstances or poor judgment, but is completely willing and able to fully go along with the M-type's decisions on everything. But this is not the situation we're referring to.)

It is also true that partners should not be each other's therapists. You're just not objective enough. Declaring yourself a master does not make you necessarily more impartial and excuse you from that basic rule. If you are someone's lover and believe that you can be wholly objective about them, you are fooling yourself.

Before we go further, I want to make it clear that I'm not trying to come down on people with mental illnesses as unworthy beings who shouldn't be in any relationship, much less a power dynamic. I know quite a few s-types with mental illnesses who are in quite successful power dynamic relationships—and for that matter, a number of M-types as well. (For direct advice on how this can be done, check out the books *Broken Toys* and *Mastering Mind*, in the appendix at the back of the book.) However, the s-types in these situations had more experienced riders, as it were. Taking any responsibility for someone who has an uncontrolled mental illness requires a huge amount of professional help, and a steep learning curve that you can't grasp alone. Such individuals are in a doubly vulnerable position, and an inexperienced master does them no favors to promise help they can't deliver. In fact, it sets both of you up for failure. It's actually kinder to tell them honestly that you don't feel skilled enough to manage them and their complications.

Of course, sometimes the new M-type doesn't know there's something wrong until they're well into the relationship and everything starts to crash down around them. Some s-types are not aware of their problems, or are in denial about them. Some cognitive problems, by their very nature, cause the sufferer to be unaware of the symptoms, or unable to see that they are dysfunctional. Some are afraid that if they are honest, they will be rejected, a fear that is not unfounded.

Sometimes a severe medical problem occurs after the relationship is already established, requiring a rethinking of the entire structure. Figuring out that there's a problem, and whether it's a problem that you can handle, isn't easy. There's no specific way to tell, because people, problems, and relationships are all different. However, here are a few suggestions made by various experienced M-types who've been through this:

1) When they are in an emotional state, they lose the ability to obey simple orders like "Sit down" or "Shut up" or "Pick that up", or repeating a simple phrase. Warning signs should not be only that they choose to disobey, but that they honestly become unable to make themselves obey. Justifying their lack of self-control later—"Well, you made me lose control!"—is another warning sign. (Problems with more complicated orders such as modulating their tone of voice, or problem-solving or introspection when in a heightened emotional state, is more understandable. Those can be dealt with later.)

2) They cannot manage to obey and follow rules when unsupervised. When you're gone, so is their motivation. Some rules could reasonably be a struggle for anyone, but if they can't even stick to simple, basic rules when you're gone—especially around compulsive behaviors—that's a warning sign.

3) They frequently fail to do ordinary "adulting" activities such as paying their bills, maintaining personal hygiene, behaving appropriately in public, etc. They can't seem to manage their own affairs in a way that doesn't have them constantly living crisis to crisis. (If you are confident that you understand why they are struggling with this, and you are willing to provide parental-level supervision and support, this might be able to work. But in conjunction with other emotional issues, this can indicate a situation which is beyond the ability of a master to control.)

4) They lie or deliberately deceive you or others who trust them.

5) They are very secretive about their home life, their background, or their online activity. When people are just starting to get to know each other, a certain amount of discretion is normal. However, as both people get to know each other, the s-type should be at least working toward transparency. Refusing to be honest about potions of one's life can point toward addiction problems, or at least toward someone with huge trust issues that will need special handling, probably with outside help.

6) They can't have a reasonable conversation about ex-lovers— the stories seem implausible, or change frequently, or immediately send them into a bad emotional spiral that takes a long time to get out of. They can't answer the question "What was going on in your head when that was happening?" If they tell you that every one of their ex-lovers was a horrible abuser, at the very least this will be a very damaged person.

7) They misremember the past in dramatically slanted ways. (This can get very dangerous, even if most heavy discussions are written down or in emails. It can eventually lead to the M-type being accused of betraying their trust, breaking "promises", or violating their consent. Obviously if you haven't been around this person for very long, you won't know what they are misremembering, but it's something to note. We aren't talking about forgetting little things here, but remembering an incident extremely differently from what actually happened and in a very negative way, or interpreting offhand statements as "promises".

8) Their opinions of people change from white to black with no seeming ability to see shades of nuance, with no realistic understanding of why a person might have done this thing, except that they are a horrible person or want the s-type to suffer, etc. They either can't or won't try to see the situation from another person's point of view.

9) You perceive a problem and point it out, and they are not willing to accept or believe it. Understand that you are not likely to be able to convince them just because you both decide

that you are their master. (You could be wrong, of course. But look at how they respond to it. Do they hear the actual points you are making and show some insight into their own mental/emotional process, or do they twist it around into something entirely different?)

10) They are unable to handle you pointing out their mistakes or correcting them—they may argue every point, or dissolve into tears, or launch into a torrent of self-criticism. Most s-types won't do well on a steady diet of the type of harsh treatment and verbal abuse found in pornography or S/M scenes, but if you find yourself hesitant to give any correction at all for fear of their emotional reactions, it will undermine any feeling of authority.

11) They are violent, or threaten violence, or intentionally destroy your property. Even if they are physically incapable of doing much real damage to you, slapping or kicking you in anger is a sign something is seriously wrong. Also, attempting to restrain them when they are physically out of control can lead to accidentally injury.

12) They threaten to "expose you", or get your children taken away, for your involvement in BDSM or M/s, even if the threats are unrealistic or said in the heat of the moment and they later apologize.

I'm speaking from experience here. Of the various s-types I've had before, one's mental illness recurred a couple of years into our dynamic. It was rough going, but we were able to figure out a way and get through it. We had to fight our way through his disappointment that I couldn't "master" him out of it, and my futile attempts to do so, but once we'd gotten that out of our systems we managed to get him some help and we muddled through. He remained largely self-aware through it, and was definitely willing to acknowledge his disorder and commit to doing whatever was necessary to work with it.

However, I've had other s-types come to me with various issues, some of them definitely above my pay grade to handle—in time, energy, and most importantly understanding and skill in knowing how to cope with it. Most of those broke up quickly, but at least one went on for some years, only getting worse while I doggedly hung on. He was in therapy, but would not discuss it with me and refused couples counseling for us. I kept pressing on, assuming that I would be able to find a way to manage him around his issues without professional help, but eventually I had to acknowledge that it was beyond my current ability to handle. I also had to acknowledge that my inability to admit to that as soon as it began to be apparent had caused more harm to both of us. Eventually the relationship, and the power dynamic, deteriorated and broke up.

So what if you're facing down someone whom you like, but who may be more than you can handle from an authority perspective? Here are questions to ask, some for yourself and some for them.

1) What does their support system look like? Do they have useful therapy, ideally with a professional who specializes in their issue? If not, are they open to getting some? Do they have friends or family or a support group? Or are they hoping that you'll carry the whole load of being their support system?

2) Do they expect that being in a power dynamic with "fix" any of the problems that are associated with their disorder(s)? If so, you will have to convince them that this is unrealistic. You'll have to convince yourself as well—it can be very seductive to want to "save" an s-type.

3) Do you have the time and energy to put into a relationship that will likely take up a lot more of both than an average power dynamic? Rather than thinking of it as the amount of time and effort you'd put into a romantic partner, think of it as the amount of time and effort you'd put into a high-need child, or a new puppy. This is an adult, but the commitment can be significantly more effort than that of an s-type without serious problems. This is also the moment to ask yourself what role you expect the s-type to have—that of a responsible adult partner, or of a high-need child?

4) We strongly feel that particularly severe problems such as addictions, eating disorders, compulsive self-harmful or violent

behavior, or personality disorders, will probably be above your pay grade to handle without professional help for both of you. These disorders are considered to be challenging for mental health professionals to handle; there's no shame in backing down from that. If you really want to take on someone with those issues, they need to be in therapy, *you* need to be in therapy just to have a separate support system to vent to who understands the gravity of the situation, and you have to be able to meet with their therapist periodically to work through the problems that will come up between you. It's not necessary to tell the therapist that you are their master—you can just be a very supportive partner who wants to know how to best help them—but if you want to take that leap, we recommend giving the therapist the book *Unequal By Design: Counseling Power Dynamic Relationships* (found in the appendix).

5) If their behavior (and their ability to obey rules) deteriorates when they are unsupervised … well, how much time do you have? Do you have the time and energy to give them constant supervision? Do not assume that supervision will make their self-control any better. In fact, it may do the opposite, depending on the situation.

6) Consider your own risk profile. Not all M-types are unscathed when it comes to trauma or brain issues. Does their crazy fit badly with your crazy? If you're hotheaded and they're very emotionally sensitive, or if you need a lot of alone time and they're very needy, or if they want to be a brat and you need gentle respect, it's not going to go well. This doesn't mean that they will be a deal-breaker for everyone, but they will be for you.

7) Remember that some formerly abused individuals unconsciously seek out people whose personal characteristics resemble their abusers in some way. If your flaws resemble those, even on a much smaller level that wouldn't be considered "abusive" by other people, they may unconsciously want to cast you in that story in order to live it out again. That's a bad place for an M-type to be, for many reasons. Are they willing or able

to honestly communicate that information to you, so that you can assess this risk? (Recounting the personal characteristics of an abuser and honestly discussing whether you have them is not the same as recounting the abuse itself.)

8) Think about what your actual dealbreakers are, and stick to them. Lying? Stealing, from you or others? Sexually inappropriate behavior around your children? Physical violence? Verbal abuse? Use of drugs? Illegal activity such as nonviolent crime? Careless indiscretion with names or phone numbers? Self-harm? People often start out on their "best behavior", and things deteriorate gradually. Whatever your deal-breakers may me, consider what it would be like to get heavily emotionally invested in the relationship, and then face one of these. It is very tempting to make excuses for the bad behavior of people we love, which leads to a very bad place for both people. Do you have experience with giving "tough love" and setting firm boundaries with people you care about? If you are at risk for feeling pressured by strong emotions or pity or emotional "sunk cost", this may be a bad fit for you.

9) For that matter, can you hold to calm, reasonable boundaries in the face of irrational emotional behavior … over and over and over? What will you do to keep from becoming overstressed? Do you have people to turn to who will be understanding about your insistence on sticking to this relationship? One of the often-unspoken problems of taking on a partner with behavioral issues is that one's friends and family, who may be seeing only a simplistic version of the situation, may not be overly supportive when you are having difficulty with the partner. Take the time to lineup some more neutral support, including a therapist of your own, if you are determined to do this. Remember that you are not necessarily alone in the world. Your partner's behavior will not only affect you, but it will affect other people in your life. They may act in ways that will hurt or upset your friends and family. Other people may think badly of you, blaming you for your s-type's problems or

criticizing the way you handle them. Your friends may think badly of your s-type, or want to protect you from them.

Again, if you're reading this and you're an s-type with issues like these—or the M-type of such an s-type—and you're thinking, "But we found a way to work through this, and now we're stronger than ever, and very glad that we stuck it out with each other!" … that's terrific. I honor and respect your commitment, persistence, understanding, self-awareness, and all the other great qualities you probably had to engage in order to make it happen. Before you get offended, though, I want you to think of one of your friends who doesn't have as many of those necessary qualities, and who decides tomorrow that they want to own a slave … and think of them attempting to master an s-type just like the one in your relationship. If you just winced, you'll understand why I'm including this essay in this book.

Mastery is risk assessment, as quoted from another essay here. One of the risks in the equation is you, and how far you are willing and able to go before you can no longer manage being in charge … or, for that matter, how long before mastery is no longer a positive part of your life and relationship, but is instead a painful, stressful burden. If you're not an experienced rider, you may want to choose a somewhat less advanced-level horse—for both your sake and theirs.

# Mastering Through Feminist Guilt
*Nysa Freehand*

Most people, in and out of the lifestyle, complain that the biggest problem with new would-be masters is that they are all narcissistic, selfish, and probably sexist idiots who think being a master means they won't have to do any work in a relationship, and can just get everything their way at a demand. While I'm not arguing that I haven't met those people, this isn't the only problem that needs to be talked about. Some of us come to mastery with the opposite problem—or boatload of problems. I did, and there was no one around who could address my issues for a very long time.

I consider myself a lesbian-feminist, and I've been active in movements of feminism, women's spirituality, nonviolence, and other radical causes for the past thirty years or so, ever since I came out in my early twenties and leaped with idealistic spirit into trying to make the world better. Between the ages of twenty and thirty, I was head-down in the ideology that all groups should be leaderless and work by consensus, and that no human being should be allowed to control another. (Well, OK, I deliberately didn't think about whether that should include violent criminals. I was a little naïve and I didn't think a lot of points all the way through.) Having control over another person, or at least another adult, would not have been on my radar as ethically feasible at that time.

At the age of thirty I discovered BDSM. At first I tried to be a bottom, because I was ashamed to admit that I was really drawn to topping, and afraid that if I set foot onto that shore I would be swept away by abusive desires that would lead me to harming someone. When I finally made that transition, I discovered that those fears were entirely ungrounded in reality. I'm quite able to tell fantasy from reality, to judge what is harmful, and to keep myself from doing things I know are a bad idea. I think that some of the rhetoric I read had primed me to believe that if someone had even a few desires that vaguely resembled abuse, they were a monster ready to explode outward into mayhem and the only ethical choice would be to repress and hopefully purge those feelings.

Twice I bought BDSM toys with the intent of using them on a willing partner (and I had three lovely women who'd offered to help me with my "topping cherry"). Twice I gave them all away. Finally, an older leatherdyke I respected pointed out that the language I was using to describe my fears around topping sounded an awful lot like the language my homophobic parents used around my sexual preference. I realized that although I'd fortunately long since gotten over my internalized homophobia, I'd shifted those feelings and projected them onto my BDSM longing, which were unacceptable not only to my parents but to the progressive communities I was a part of. Finally, something I could flagellate myself for which would ingratiate me to the finger-shakers on both teams! When I realized this, I sheepishly called up one of the aforementioned lovely bottoms and, with a quaver in my voice, arranged to lose my "topping cherry". She was a wonderful ice cream sundae and I walked away feeling far more confident and trusting in myself, and my self-control. I remember driving home and mentally testing myself, just to make sure that a couple of hours of wielding a whip hadn't turned me into a ravening psychopath. Nope, still me. I was relieved.

But of course BDSM stops at the end of the negotiated scene and doesn't push itself into everyday life. This was the new boundary I drew for myself, putting "good" on one side of it and "bad" on the other side. As long as it was just kinky play—and long as it wasn't *real*—everything was fine. That lasted until I was almost forty, and my partner (and bottom) of three years suggested that she wanted to be my slave. I resisted the idea. It was true that being her top had done amazing things for my confidence and centeredness—I was better at calmly holding boundaries, facing down difficult situations, and taking on new challenges. In a lot of ways, it had begun unfolding my dominant self, which frightened me. I was back to worrying that wanting to be a leader, to be in charge of people, was not an ethical way to be. I turned down multiple leadership opportunities that were offered to me because of these fears. Finally, more out of exasperation than anything else (but isn't that so often the case) I picked up the abandoned leadership role in a local non-profit organization whose cause I cared about. Within a year I was commanding three teams of people who answered to me, and being paid for it (although certainly not enough to make me rich).

I learned a lot about managing people that year. In order for me to do my job effectively, I had to actively learn leadership and management skills, which meant that I had to believe it was possible to do this effectively and ethically. I took a lot of trainings; I expected that leadership training would all be either some sort of pseudo-military jackbooted stuff or a course in "how to be a ruthless CEO". While I did see some of those out there, I also found courses by thoughtful and progressive people I came to respect, and learned a lot about what responsive leadership actually looked like. The non-profit I worked for was so happy to keep me in the job that they enthusiastically supported (and paid for) these classes.

During the period that I was taking these classes, my partner would periodically bring up the idea that if I could do this for my job, couldn't I do this for my relationship? I would always decline. I couldn't say what I was really thinking, which was that it was awfully tempting, but I was afraid that it would be politically incorrect. Instead of honestly stating my fears, I pompously told her that it was important that she "empower herself" and become an assertive person who wouldn't want to be in a subordinate role. (Man, am I grateful now that she continued to put up with me.)

Ironically, it was one of the teachers who trained me in ethical leadership who changed my mind. At one point during the training, he made an offhand comment about how he was head of his household and used these leadership skills at home as well as at work. I immediately assumed that he was some straight guy who kept his wife at home and ran their lives according to unexamined "traditional values". However, later in the class it came out that he was actually gay, and that knocked my stereotypical assumptions for a loop. After class I came up to him and hesitantly asked him how, if he was queer, he could bring power-over into his home. We ended up talking for two hours in a café, where he described his life as a Leather master with two male slaves, and how he tried to steward their lives as he would a well-run ethical business or interest group or piece of sacred land. Actually, when he said the word "sacred land", something in my chest felt like it snapped, and I haltingly described my girlfriend's desires, and my own ambivalence.

He pointed out that if I was withholding my mastery from her for the reasons I was stating, I was already deciding who she was and what was best for her, regardless of her own stated needs—a very dominant act, and not a very ethical one at that. I pointed out that I couldn't believe that a healthy person would really want to be a subordinate. He told me that it was normal for dominant types to have a hard time relating to the reality of a submissive type, because it was so far beyond our experience of anything we'd find desirable. However, he pointed out, it was important to accept someone's own evaluation of who they are at their core, or we are not respecting their identity and self-assessment. Using one's self as a touchstone for what is healthy for everyone else in the world is a self-centered position, he told me, and not worthy of an ethical leader. *We have to meet people where they are and not project ourselves onto them,* he said.

My cheeks flamed and I admitted my fears around political correctness. He gently told me that no one outside gets the right to tell him, or his partners, or by extension me and mine, how we ought to run our relationships. He asked if I felt that I had a good ethical compass and the ability to discern whether any given interaction was actively hurting or harming someone. I replied that I believed I did have that sense. *Well then,* he said, *instead of looking to other people's general principles, why don't you try being the leader in your relationship and depend on that sense?*

Over the next year, he became my mentor in power exchange. When I went home that night, confessed everything to my partner, and told her that I was now willing to try this out, she surprised me by dropping to her knees and kissing my feet. I was caught so hard between conflicting feelings—"Isn't this somehow wrong?" and "Oh, I want this so much!"—that I actually started crying. I slowly got over the first feeling, over the next year, and came fully into the second one.

We have been master and slave for seven years now. (I prefer the term "master" to "mistress" because I'm not terribly femmy, and that word feels femmy to me.) It's likely that most would-be masters may be shaking their heads reading this, or laughing at me, or even sneering.

It's possible. But there may be a few out there who will recognize themselves. Let me tell you that my politics haven't changed all that much. I still support most of the same causes. I'm still a feminist, and so is my slave. I am one hundred per cent behind the various civil rights—human rights—movements that I've supported for many years. I am against laws that take away people's right to consent, and I think that my journey has given me a much more complex and nuanced understanding of what consent is.

Before I accepted who and what I am, I had to accept who and what my beloved is, which meant accepting her understanding of herself without judging her experience as wrong or unhealthy, just because I didn't understand it. That broadening of my understanding has reverberated out into many other areas of my life. I found myself examining the self-stories of people I'd worked with or marched next to or just heard about, stories I'd judged in one way or another as them fooling themselves about some part of their experience. My enculturated mind told me, "If they only knew what I knew, they wouldn't have that identity." Finally accepting my partner's self-story at face value, trusting her to know herself, and really listening to her lived internal experience pushed me to be more objective and nonjudgmental about many other people in my life. Accepting my own internal experience taught me how often I've judged from a place of fear, which so often distorts what we see. I've learned that it is not a loving act to deny someone's experience of themselves just because it makes you uncomfortable.

Yes, you can be a feminist and be a master—or a slave. Feminism is first and foremost about choice—at least the feminism that I practice is about choice—and giving people fair and equal choices, whenever humanly possible. If one person chooses to follow a trusted other, that choice should be respected. If the other person chooses to accept the great gift and frightening responsibility of constantly struggling to be an ethical leader, every day of their life so long as they hold this position, that choice should be accepted. I might even say that it should be celebrated. Both should, really.

And yes, people are going to make mistakes. They make mistakes already, with egalitarian relationships. This style of loving together will be no exception. But as this book hopefully imparts, the answer has to be education. If the information exists on how to manage these pairings, and if people can find it, we can at least work toward harm reduction. The answer to "What will my progressive political community think of me?" is also education. Just like every other minority, we have to speak up—carefully and thoughtfully—and show just how much we are not like unthinking "traditional" relationships based on models of oppression. Because we certainly don't have to be that. I have no problem basing my mastery on values of fairness and compassion. You can do the same, you who are reading this book.

It is true that as someone who is highly invested in social justice, I feel a stronger calling to get this right, to be a responsible steward and not an unthinking oppressor, to check myself and get checks from people I respect on a regular basis. That just means I have to try harder and be more self-aware, which is good for my personal growth anyway. One thing I've learned is that good leaders listen—not just to what their subordinates say, but to what is not being said. We listen and we respond to what's going on. Working with my slave is actually easier than working with the people at my job, because of her transparency requirement. I don't have to guess; I can just ask. But I have to be willing to ask, and not be afraid of what she's going to say. I have to trust that we're both smart adults and we can figure this out together.

I've come a long way since I faced down my internalized discomfort around my BDSM practices. Now I see the trend, and I watch for it. I was told that being a lesbian was unhealthy, and that to be healthy I should push myself away from it. Then I got my first lover and learned just how much nonsense that was. I was told the same thing about BDSM, and once I had a partner who enjoyed it, I learned the same lesson. I went down that road all over again with M/s. How many times will I have to do that? Next time I'm told that something I love and long for is sick, will I remember to immediately seek out the people who are doing it and observe them, see if they're happy—and if they are, discard my assumptions and jump in? I hope so.

Becoming a master has changed me and made me grow as a person. I'm more responsible, because I have to be in order to make this work. I'm more confident, which came as a side benefit. I'm also, paradoxically, more humble, because the process of getting here taught me more about myself and my assumptions. I hope that it continues to push me to grow, and that it does the same for you.

---

*Nysa Freehand is a Leatherdyke Master who lives in Arizona with her slave/partner, a dog and three cats. She works for an environmental protection organization and knits.*

# The Attributes of Leadership
*Sir Guy de Brownsville*

We have many conversations about the type of hierarchical relationships we pursue or with which we are involved, but intrinsic to any authority-based relationship is the concept of leadership. We are constantly inundated with conversations about it, ideologies surrounding it, complaints about the quality of it and cries for more of it. Why is that? Why is leadership so important to us?

It is because it is built into our lifestyle. Whether it is within our personal relationships, in our secular worlds, or in our communities, effective leadership can make things better and defective leadership can make things miserable. It makes no difference whether we identify as Dominant or submissive, Owner or property, Master or slave; we all have a role in one way or another that requires leadership. Though this particular discussion may seem to be focused on the Masters and Owners, the subjects we are going to discuss are attributes that are not isolated to those on that side of the slash. It is true, however, that leadership is crucial for anyone who would attempt to lead a household.

To make sure we are all on the same page, let us make sure we're speaking of the same thing. What exactly is leadership? How would you define it? If you were to look at the dictionary definition of leadership, you would find several permutations of the word "leader" repeated. The synonyms listed give us a start: *administration, management, directorship, control, governorship, stewardship, hegemony, authoritativeness, influence, command, effectiveness; sway, clout.*

In our discussion, we are going to utilize three sources which may seem not to be related at all, but as we investigate further, we will find a great deal of similarity. The three sources are the military, the business or corporate world, and religion or spirituality. We will discuss them separately and then we will cull the common points and use them as a guide. No need for trepidation—trust me, it will work!

Why would we look toward the military? Modern Leather history points us in the direction of the military with its origins. Many of the principles learned in the military and internalized during World Wars I and II formed the basis of the early Leather clubs and organizations.

While there are a variety of leadership schools in the various branches of the military, I am partial to the model for leadership given to the officers of the United States Marine Corps. From the United States Marine Corps "Leadership Traits for an Officer". *The Marine Officer's Guide, Sixth Edition,* by Lt. Col. Kenneth Estes.

❖ Be technically and tactically proficient.
❖ Know yourself and seek improvement.
❖ Know your Marines and look out for their welfare.
❖ Keep your Marines informed.
❖ Set the example.
❖ Ensure the task is understood, supervised and accomplished.
❖ Train your Marines as a team.
❖ Make sound and timely decisions.
❖ Develop a sense of responsibility in your subordinates.
❖ Employ your unit in accordance with its capabilities.
❖ Seek responsibility and take responsibility for your actions.

To summarize, in order to lead, one must possess the knowledge and skills necessary to lead. One cannot be expected to critique another's performance if one does not possess the accurate knowledge and skill required to do so. As a leader, you have to be in touch with yourself and understand that your own growth and development is never complete. One must always strive for improvement. You have never reached your pinnacle. There is always more you can learn.

To lead, you have got know and understand those in your charge. You must do what is best for them and look out for their welfare, sometimes against their own best interests. In fact, doing what is best for them may mean that you may have to sacrifice a bit of yourself or your preferences.

Keeping the people in your charge informed is important. Merely and repeatedly saying they should do a thing "…because I said so", does not instill confidence in leadership. In fact, it can undermine it. People often operate better when they know, not only what is expected of them, but why it is important or necessary.

Setting an example is also important for a leader. The "do as I say, not as I do" model gets tired quickly and that type of attitude does much to subvert the development of confidence in leadership. It makes every instruction seem like an exercise of ego.

In addition to giving instruction, there are things one in the lead must do in order to ensure success. You must ask yourself: *Were my instructions clear and concise? Did I make sure they were understood? Did I check periodically on the process and make sure there were no questions or obstacles preventing its completion? Did I make sure that it was completed and did I give praise when it was done?*

Whether leading more than one individual or whether it is just one other, do you make them feel as if they are part of a team? Developing the concept of a team working together toward a common goal helps in many ways. It allows those in your charge to feel invested in the mission and goal. It forms a sense of cohesion and purpose. It also ensures that the right tools and training will be involved to be able to reach your common goals successfully.

Decisiveness is also noted as a key ingredient to the recipe for leadership. Indecision can cause those in your charge to lose confidence in your ability to lead. By being knowledgeable about the situation and any variables involved, and having confidence in your own decision-making capability, you can make timely decisions which increase the feeling of security your followers have in your leadership, as opposed to hesitating until you have a perfect plan.

It is also important to develop a sense of responsibility in those in our charge. If a person in our charge totally abdicates all responsibility, not only can there be chaos, but one can lose out on their own skill and expertise. Encouraging a sense of responsibility in those we lead allows them some agency and gives them initiative to achieve. General Patton said, "Don't tell a person what to do. Tell them what want done and you'll be amazed by their ingenuity." By doing this, not only do you help them to build self-confidence, but they will also feel that you have confidence in them, and that will build their respect for you.

When we say, "Employ your unit in accordance with its capabilities," we mean to work within the parameters of the skillsets of the person(s) that you are leading. For example, if you have someone who is a certified public accountant, you might be better served giving them tasks that involve managing finances than say, doing woodworking or gardening. If someone is a skilled carpenter, using them in a strictly clerical or administrative capacity would probably not be the best for all involved. This is not to say that one cannot or should not be trained in other skills. It does say that one should utilize the skills that they are best suited for in order to have the most success.

Finally, the Marine officer is instructed to seek responsibility and take responsibility for their actions. Again, the idiom comes into play, "Everyone wants to be in charge; no one wants to be responsible." All too often people are enamored with the idea of being in charge. They like the idea of being looked up to, of having people subordinate to them and of giving commands. But when it comes down to taking responsibility for those commands, especially when things go awry, you may find that they are reticent. They may make excuses—or worse—blame those in their charge for any failures or mistakes. Leaders take responsibility. Famously, Harry S. Truman, as President of the United States, had a sign on his desk saying, "The buck stops here." He understood that anything that happened under his administration, good or bad, would end up on his desk. When we take on this responsibility, we will have the respect, admiration and loyalty of those in our charge.

Field Marshal Bernard Law Montgomery defines leadership in this way: "The capacity and the will to rally men and women to a common purpose and the character which inspires confidence." He further says, "The leader must know what he himself wants. He must give firm guidance and a clear lead … It is a mistake to think that once an order is given there is nothing more to be done; you have got to see that it is carried out in the spirit in which you intended."

General Matthew Ridgway expressed in his memoir *Soldier* that a leader may utilize a staff but ultimately, he is in command and takes responsibility. He believed in discipline, tough training, and instilling a sense of pride and camaraderie in the unit. He further said that he was attentive to their morale and took care of those in his charge. He believed in being present, particularly during stressful times, to raise morale and to follow up on orders.

Now let's look at the corporate world and see what they say about the attributes of a good leader. Forbes magazine of December

2012 came out with an article by Tanya Prive that listed the top ten qualities of a great leader. According to this Forbes article, those attributes are:

- ❖ Honesty
- ❖ Ability to Delegate
- ❖ Ability to Inspire
- ❖ Sense of Humor
- ❖ Confidence
- ❖ Commitment
- ❖ Positive Attitude
- ❖ Creativity
- ❖ Intuition
- ❖ Communication

*"The secret of war lies in the communications."* –Napoleon Bonaparte

Already we can see some similarities in the military model of the attributes of leadership and the corporate model—even if, in today's corporate world, we may not seem to see these qualities immediately manifest in those who lead the world's corporations. But let's look at a further definition of the attributes of leadership according to the Center on Congress at Indiana University. They list the following:

- ❖ Energy
- ❖ Vision
- ❖ Self confidence
- ❖ Takes responsibility
- ❖ Judgment
- ❖ Decisive
- ❖ Motivator
- ❖ People skills
- ❖ Actor
- ❖ Relationship with followers
- ❖ Moral leadership: Moral leadership means being trustworthy and fulfilling one's commitments. It means working for the common good. It means living up to, promoting, and defending the laws, customs and values that animate our country.

According to inc.com, there are nine attributes of the corporate leader. They are as follows:

❖ *Awareness:* Understands the difference between management and employees.
❖ *Decisiveness:* Makes tough decisions.
❖ *Empathy:* Genuine concern for others.
❖ *Accountability:* Takes responsibility for everyone's performance, including their own.
❖ *Confidence:* Confidence is contagious. Employees are naturally drawn to them, seek their advice, and feel more confident as a result.
❖ *Optimism:* A source of positive energy.
❖ *Honesty:* Treating people the way they want to be treated; extremely ethical.
❖ *Focus:* Plans ahead, supremely organized; thinks through multiple scenarios and the possible impacts of their decisions.
❖ *Inspiration:* Motivates everyone to give his or her best all the time. They challenge their people by setting high but attainable standards and expectations, and then giving them the support, tools, training, and latitude to pursue those goals.

Again, in all of these corporate models, we can see significant overlap with the military model described in more detail at the onset. But I would also like to explore the attributes of leadership that are established in some religious or spiritual communities. While we cannot possibly cover every belief system and what philosophy they espouse as far as leadership is concerned, we can take a small sample which will give us a good idea of what attributes are deemed to be important in those who would lead.

Let us start with Christianity. Many of the concepts of leadership in Christianity come from the numerous letters of Paul to the Christian congregations and to a protégé, Timothy, who was himself a relatively novice leader in the congregation according to theologians. We can start with Paul's letter to Titus in Titus 1:7-14, (ESV):

> *For an overseer, as God's steward, must be above reproach. He must not be arrogant or quick-tempered or a drunkard or*

*violent or greedy for gain, but hospitable, a lover of good, self-controlled, upright, holy, and disciplined. He must hold firm to the trustworthy word as taught, so that he may be able to give instruction in sound doctrine and also to rebuke those who contradict it. For there are many who are insubordinate, empty talkers and deceivers ... They must be silenced, since they are upsetting whole families by teaching for shameful gain what they ought not to teach.*

Let's now look at his letter to Timothy with regards to the qualifications for overseers, or elders, and deacons or ministerial servants. 1 Timothy 3:1-5 reads as follows:

*Here is a trustworthy saying: Whoever aspires to be an overseer desires a noble task. Now the overseer is to be above reproach, faithful to his wife, temperate, self-controlled, respectable, hospitable, able to teach, not given to drunkenness, not violent but gentle, not quarrelsome, not a lover of money. He must manage his own family well and see that his children obey him, and he must do so in a manner worthy of full respect. (If anyone does not know how to manage his own family, how can he take care of God's church?)*

So in these two scriptures we find these common attributes: He says they must be above reproach. They must, therefore, have a good reputation in the community. In a variety of ways, it articulates the type of temperament that is expected. An overseer or elder is expected to be calm and disciplined. Self-control is mentioned in both texts, as is the ability to teach. Indeed, if one is to lead, they must also be able to give instruction and help others to learn, so having teaching ability is instrumental to this. Honesty is also noted, as the texts say they must not be deceivers or empty talkers. Being hospitable is also emphasized in both texts, meaning one must be approachable, humble, and have the ability to put someone at ease. It speaks of not being arrogant or quarrelsome, and both also caution against the abuse of alcohol. Finally, it says that such a person should be in control of their own household in addition to being in control of themselves, with the side note that if they cannot lead their own household, how can they be expected to do so with the congregation?

Going from Christianity to Islam, we have to understand that Islam, another of the Abrahamic religions, recognizes the Torah, or "Injil", as well as the Qu'ran. In addition to the Qur'an, there are *hadiths*, which are the sayings and traditions of the Prophet Muhammad compiled by his companions. They can be likened to the Torah and the Talmud in Judaism. Islamic *hadith*, as well as the Qur'an, speak about hierarchical relationships. In doing so, they recognize that many people have within themselves the ability to lead, though they may not find themselves in leadership positions per se. They also warn of those thirsty to be in positions of power but who are not fit to lead. One such *hadith* from Sufyān al-Thawrī reads, "From what I have seen, the one thing that people are least willing to give up is the desire to become a leader of others. You will see a person give up eating and drinking (excessively); he will abandon wealth and (expensive) clothing. But when we assign him a position of leadership, he stands up and becomes antagonistic and defensive (and ambitious)".

While the literal definition of "muslim" is "one who submits," Islam also teaches about leadership and its attributes, and clearly defines the qualities that are expected in one who leads. Key to this is the belief that any authority they may have over another is a gift from God or Allah, and that one in a position of authority is, therefore, a representative of Allah. That said, such a person must be considered worthy of that honor, and is to represent the qualities and attributes of Allah and of his faithful servants. The Qu'ran states this when it says, "It is He Who hath made you (His) agents, inheritors of the earth: He hath raised you in ranks, some above others: that He may try you in the gifts He hath given you: for thy Lord is quick in punishment: yet He is indeed Oft-forgiving, Most Merciful." (Al-An'âm 6: 165)

In his dissertation, "Islamic Leadership Principles: A Success Model for Everyone and All Times", Dr. Adalat Khan breaks down the attributes of leadership from an Islamic perspective. He describes these principles of leadership as follows:

❖ Faith and belief.
❖ Knowledge and wisdom.
❖ Courage and determination.
❖ Mutual consultation and unity. (Fraternity and brotherhood.)
❖ Morality and piety. (Honesty and trust.)
❖ Superior communication.
❖ Justice and compassion.

❖ Patience and endurance.
❖ Commitment and sacrifice.
❖ Lifelong endeavour.
❖ Gratitude and prayers.

Having a strong moral compass and being firmly rooted in the faith is important within the principles of Islamic leadership. The idea that the Qur'an is their basis and that Prophet Muhammad is the best example is a fundamental component to leadership. It sets a standard and a guiding set of principles to abide by.

The idea that knowledge (which is the acquiring, processing and assimilation of information) and wisdom (which is about taking that information and making a prudent practical application of it) are mentioned as requirements or principles of leadership, is not surprising. If one is to guide another, the ability to receive information and wisely utilize it is important.

Because leaders face adversity and have to overcome obstacles, one must be determined. One must also have courage because sometimes the choices that may be the best ones are not the popular ones. Also, a leader must face adversity head on if they expect the respect of those that they lead.

When one views the people they lead as part of a team (or a family), they will not lord it over those in their charge. There is a saying, "I want for my brother what I want for myself." A leader is not selfish but looks out for those in their charge, treating them as they themselves would wish to be treated. A leader will consider the expertise and knowledge of those in their charge, sometimes even soliciting their thoughts before making decisions. In this way they forge the idea among their followers that they, too, are invested in the outcome as they strive to achieve a common goal together.

Being a person of integrity—one worthy of trust—is a principle also stressed in Islamic leadership principles. Leading by example is important. It is difficult for one to follow someone who does not set an example of honesty or who does not inspire trust. It leads to trepidation and can undermine the leader's authority.

Just as we say repeatedly in this lifestyle, communication is important according to the principles of Islamic leadership. However, we're not just talking about communication, but about effective communication. Being clear and concise is key. A leader must make sure that they are understood, but they must also seek to understand those in their charge. Communication is recognized as a two-way street.

Being just and fair goes hand in hand with showing compassion. No one wants to follow someone who is a tyrant, who consistently shows they don't have your best interest at heart. Having the flexibility to understand that mistakes can be made and to be able to deal with setbacks in a concerned and compassionate manner can solidify the confidence of those that you lead. If they are certain that you will deal with them in a manner that is fair, they will be able to accept discipline when it comes.

To do this requires patience and endurance. The role of leadership is not an easy task. It can be a protracted struggle. In fact, the Qu'ran teaches that struggle is ordained and just as a strong sword is forged by fire and the blows of the hammer, so a strong leader is forged by struggle and adversity. Having the perseverance to come through adversity and the patience to see things through during rough times are skills critical in forging the qualities of a leader.

Sacrifice and commitment are an integral part of leadership in Islam. Part of a key Islamic prayer recited daily uses the words of the Prophet Muhammad as recorded in the Qu'ran in Sura al-An'am, verse 162: "My prayers, my sacrifice, my life and my death, are for Allah the Lord of the worlds." The concept of self-sacrifice is important in Islam and, as such, is also just as important to one who would lead in Islam. Being committed to the cause and being able and willing to make sacrifices to promote it are important leadership principles. In order to look out for those in their charge, a leader may have to put their own comfort aside. It is part of how they show commitment so that those in their charge will take their own commitment seriously.

Being a leader also means understanding that undertaking such a role is not a short-term situation. Those in leadership must be constantly striving to improve themselves, to learn and to grow. They have to invest time and effort, and this can take years. A leader has to be willing to devote themselves to the task of leadership, always trying to take it just a little further.

The final principle noted for leadership in Islam is gratitude and prayer. Essentially, it is about maintaining humility, understanding that one's place as a leader is also that of service. As noted earlier, in Islam leadership is considered a gift, and giving thanks for that gift is important because just as it is given, it can be taken away.

Since we are looking at the Abrahamic religions, let us look at Judaism and the principles of leadership outlined therein. If we were to examine the Torah (or the "Old Testament"), we will see many examples of leadership, from Abraham to Moses and Aaron, to Joshua, to King David and King Solomon. We see examples of leadership in adversity, leadership in crisis and war, as well as management under times that are not so trying.

Many remember the account of the leadership of Moses during the canonical exile in Egypt. Few remember that when first given the responsibility of leadership, Moses had a great deal of trepidation about it. According to the Common English Bible, Moses says in Exodus 4: 10, "But Moses said to the Lord, "My Lord, I've never been able to speak well, not yesterday, not the day before, and certainly not now since you've been talking to your servant. I have a slow mouth and a thick tongue." However, it is apparent that he was able to overcome both his lack of self-confidence and his public speaking ability, as later accounts show him as a bold and dynamic leader. By looking at the model of Moses, we can glean much about the principles of leadership as set out in Judaism.

Based upon this history, in an article in the Jerusalem Post, Jonathan Sacks lays out seven principles of Jewish leadership. He lists them as follows:

- ❖ Leadership begins with taking responsibility.
- ❖ No one can lead alone. Leadership is about the future. It is vision-driven.
- ❖ Leaders learn.
- ❖ Leadership means believing in the people you lead.
- ❖ Leadership involves a sense of timing and pace.
- ❖ Leadership is stressful and emotionally demanding.

Looking at the Torah, we see that though Moses was reluctant to take leadership because of his perceived limitations, once given the mantle of leadership he did not shirk responsibility but nobly took it on. This was further borne out when his loss of temper led to him being unable to enter the Promised Land. Instead of simply brooding about it, he prepared Joshua for leadership. Deuteronomy 31 indicates the Moses called Joshua in before him to pass the torch, encouraging and exhorting him, telling him to be courageous and strong.

While Moses is often the focus in much of the retelling of these accounts, the fact was that it was Moses and Aaron, his older brother, who comprised a leadership team, and there are plenty of examples of Moses consulting with Aaron and their sister Miriam. This highlights the principle that one cannot lead alone. Being able to listen to the advice of others and to get other points of view is key to making good, insightful decisions as a leader. A leader also has to have a vison for the future, and this was demonstrated by Moses preparing Joshua to lead Israel after the deaths of Miriam and Aaron.

Leaders learn. They are not content to rest on their laurels or to believe that they know enough. They are constantly in search of knowledge and wisdom. We are told that Solomon prayed for wisdom and sought it out to be able to lead effectively. One may observe on the doorposts of many Jewish homes a little box known as a *mezuzah*. These little boxes contain a verse or prayer from the Torah as a constant reminder of the presence of the Supreme Being in their lives. The Torah says in Deuteronomy that a king must write his own Sefer Torah in order to commit it to memory, and to read it daily. Also, in the first chapter of the book of Joshua, the man who assumed leadership from Moses, was commanded to meditate on the Law day and night.

In order to inspire and motivate the people in your charge, a leader must have faith in them and their ability to follow their lead. This is especially true when one reviews the early canonical history of Israel. They did not start out with kings, rather, they had prophets and chieftains and judges, all raised from among the people. The idea is that while certain ones were chosen to *lead* the people, they were not expected to *rule* the people. Coming from among the people themselves, they had to have faith in their followers in order to expect them to respect and follow their leadership.

The fact that a sense of timing and pace is needed to be considered an effective leader in this Jewish concept of leadership is borne out repeatedly throughout the account of Moses. There were times of apprehension, fear, and doubt among the people, and it took considerable time to shore them up and motivate them. It was never a one-time deal, but something which had to be done incrementally. There were times when doubts were fomented simply by the lack of the leader's physical presence.

This and many other examples show that leadership is stressful. In the Torah, we are repeatedly reminded of the difficulties in leading people. Moses had to deal with the regrets of his people after leaving Egypt; Jeremiah, Elijah, and King Solomon also had to endure difficulties. Jonah's story tells that the stress of facing the prospect of dealing with recalcitrant or unrepentant individuals caused him to flee from his work among them. The Talmud says that being tested is a part of leadership. According to Midrash Rabba Shmos 2:2, Moses was first tested in small matters, even as a shepherd after fleeing from his killing of the Egyptian. The account speaks of Moses following a young lamb which had run away from the flock. After allowing the little lamb to drink, he lifted it upon his shoulders to carry it back to safety. According to the account, this act showed that he had the right disposition to lead Israel.

So we've looked at the Abrahamic religions, and as such, it would seem logical that their principles of leadership would have similarities, given their common origin. But what if we stepped out from that genre of spiritual beliefs into another? Let us explore Buddhism and the concepts of leadership that can be gleaned from that belief system.

The uninitiated may have only a passing familiarity with Buddhism, much of which may be culled from peripheral knowledge of those who may practice it, or—unfortunately—from kung fu movies featuring Shaolin monks and martial arts. Buddhism is generally seen as a peaceful belief system of spiritual exploration and discipline, but not necessarily as one with leadership at its core. That erroneous assumption is belied by the fact it is one of the world's major religions, claiming at least 7% of the world's population. Even those who are not Buddhists are familiar with its beliefs and many of its practices.

In his treatise, "Engaged Buddhism: A Critical Analysis of Leadership Qualities in Early Buddhism", Chhen Sela states that the core values of Buddhism, of which the ultimate goal is enlightenment, is the goal of achieving "happiness, peace and development" and that becomes manifest in how each person treats another, and inspires another. These core goals are even more important for those who would lead a family, a group or an organization.

Buddhism principles around leadership and management seem like they'd be very different from Abrahamic values, but even here we can also see some similarities. Meditation, self-examination, self-exploration and adherence to a strict moral code are at the core of Buddhist beliefs. Despite some people's mental images of Buddhism, these concepts could be beneficial for those who would lead others. Practitioners of Buddhism are encouraged to develop renunciation, compassion, and superior wisdom through studying, meditating, and practicing. One of the ways in which this is manifest is in the concept known as The Four Noble Truths. These truths are:

- ❖ The truth of suffering (Dukkha), i.e., all life is suffering. That is to say, suffering is a fact of life. It is unavoidable. It is a solitary act. Though there may be those around you who can try to bring comfort, one must endure this on their own.
- ❖ The truth of the origin of suffering (Samudāya), i.e., that suffering is caused by desire. That is to say because of our pursuit of our desires and our ignorance, we can cause suffering to ourselves and those around us.
- ❖ The truth of the cessation of suffering (Nirodha), i.e., that suffering can be ended, and, through the application of the methods of self-discovery, meditation and strong values, one can end the suffering.
- ❖ The truth of the path to the cessation of suffering (Magga), i.e., that the end of suffering is nirvana or the release from the effects of karma and the cycle of death and rebirth.

The way to this goal is via the "Eight-fold Path":

- ❖ Right understanding
- ❖ Right thought
- ❖ Right speech
- ❖ Right action
- ❖ Right Livelihood
- ❖ Right effort
- ❖ Right mindfulness
- ❖ Right concentration

The Eight-fold Path is further divided into three elements: moral (speech, action, livelihood), mental (effort, mindfulness, concentration) and wisdom (understanding and thought). This includes "The Five Precepts", which are a personal code of morality, as follows:

- ❖ Abstain from destroying life
- ❖ Abstain from stealing
- ❖ Abstain from sexual misconduct
- ❖ Abstain from false speech
- ❖ Abstain from intoxicants

"Well," you may be thinking, "these concepts and principles are certainly positive, but how do they pertain to leadership and their attributes?" Rebirth, or reincarnation is part of a core belief in Buddhism. As such any views toward leadership would have to have long-term implications and include long-term goals. Having oneself rooted in a good moral foundation with a strong forward-thinking mindset can make for a successful leadership model. Let us look at how this is true by applying some of the principles and teachings of Buddha to leadership.

*"All that we are is the result of what we have thought. The mind is everything. What we think we become."*

The things that we visualize and the goals that we set affect how we move toward the future. Having the proper mindset and having vison is a key attribute for one who would find themselves in a position of leadership. In Buddhism there is a set goal and a path toward that goal.

*"If you knew what I know about the power of giving, you would not let a single meal pass with sharing it in some way."*

There are several principles at play in this simple quotation. It helps us to appreciate that a leader's job is to look out for those in their charge, and that they are able to be self-sacrificing. They lead by example, because they would give of themselves to assist another, showing an example of humility in practice. In fact, Buddha gave up material comforts and riches in order to travel and to educate others while himself seeking the path to enlightenment.

*"A jug fills drop by drop."*

Patience is a requirement, because leadership is never easy. Anyone seeking a position of leadership has to exercise patience, first in their own growth and development and then with those who would be in their charge. Little by little, step by step, one must patiently lead them to the desired goal.

*"Whoever doesn't flare up at someone who's angry wins a battle that's hard to win."*

Self-control is a necessary attribute of leadership. Any leader can find themselves dealing with very emotional issues, or with the emotions of those in their charge. If they also get emotional, nothing good can be accomplished. By remaining even-tempered and keeping their emotions in check, they can de-escalate the situation and effect a positive outcome.

*"Change is never painful—only the resistance to change is painful."*

Change is inevitable. There are always variables in life, and one must adapt to those variables. Rigidity can make things difficult to succeed in leadership; adaptability and the ability to improvise are keys to being able to lead in a positive manner.

*"Never speak harsh words, for once spoken they may return to you."*

Having a principled, calm and even gentle approach to managing people can reap great dividends. Treating those in your charge as you would like to be treated—with respect, compassion and dignity—only strengthens their desire to follow your lead. It is essential for team-building as well as for assisting personal development—not only in those who are being led, but in the leaders themselves. Selflessness helps to create and to maintain a mindset of collectivism and commonality of goal.

So even though we explored several different schools of thought and many different perspectives, in analyzing these three areas of the military, the corporate world, and religious or spiritual philosophies, there are some commonalities between them when we discuss leadership. They can be summed up as:

- ❖ **Integrity:** Being true to yourself and being consistent.
- ❖ **Inspiration:** Possessing the ability to motivate those in your charge.
- ❖ **Decisiveness:** The ability to make decisions, and take responsibility for them.
- ❖ **Self-control:** Not getting emotional, but keeping in control even under duress.
- ❖ **Empathy:** Showing sensitivity and putting yourself in another's place.
- ❖ **Morality:** The ability to do what is right.
- ❖ **Vision:** Being able to see not just the immediate but the long-term results.
- ❖ **Support:** Understanding the importance of acknowledging and validating your followers.
- ❖ **Judgment:** Discernment—the ability to choose the right course even if it's not convenient.
- ❖ **Communication:** A clear, open and honest ability to communicate is essential.
- ❖ **Sense of service:** Even as a Master, there is an element of service to those who serve us.

So, in conclusion, does this mean that we must be perfect, that we cannot make mistakes? Of course not! That would be unrealistic. What is important is that we possess the humility to admit our mistakes. We must have the integrity to admit them and to correct them. Being open and honest like that inspires those in our charge. They know we will be fair, even though things are unequal. Being focused and decisive is important for Masters, Dominants or anyone who would lead, because it keeps us on track and it does the same for those who depend upon us. We must be able to control ourselves because if we react in an emotional manner, we may make bad decisions, decisions that could damage our property irreparably. Being able to see from their point of view, showing empathy and thinking in a wise mind, helps us to keep from becoming overly analytical and to remember the human component.

Being moral, which simply means being just and being principled, is key. Seeing the big picture—having vision—gives us a better perspective than just looking at what is directly in front of us. Giving support is important, and just as important is making sure we have the proper support to be successful in our mastery. Using sound judgment is critical, but even more important is clear communication. Sometimes that means saying little and listening a lot. Finally, we must have a sense of service, because though we are owners and Masters, the bottom line is that we serve those who serve us. We provide them with an atmosphere that allows them to reach higher achievements, and it is a part of our obligation to help them in this way.

As Master Jack McGeorge said in his presentation, "Leadership Skills for Community Leaders", we must be living symbols, walking the walk. We must be buck-stoppers, making the tough decisions even though they may be unpleasant. We must be visionaries who know where we are going and why and how we will get there, and we must be team builders, uniting the community and the household in pursuit of a common cause. This is what it takes to be successful.

∎∎∎∎∎∎∎∎∎∎∎∎∎∎∎∎∎∎∎∎∎∎∎∎∎∎∎∎∎∎∎∎∎∎∎∎∎∎∎∎∎∎∎∎∎∎∎∎∎∎∎∎∎∎∎∎∎

*Sir Guy de Brownsville is a Brooklyn-born Black Leatherman, Master, and Owner. He was the 2013 International Power Exchange titleholder along with his then-partner, and he is the founder and director of The Dark Lair: BDSM Support and Education for People of Color. He was the recipient of the ONYX NY/Northeast Associate of the Year 2015 award, and the author of Sharp Interrogations: Uniform Tales of Bondage and Submission.*

# Leadership and Management
*Keziah Conway*

Is being a master more like being a leader or like being a manager? Did you even know that those two functions are different? Well, they are, and if you're a master you're going to have to learn how to be both, and when each one of these modes are more appropriate. In fact, not being able to figure out when to do either of these is one of the big mistakes I've made as a master.

There are plenty of articles you can find from the corporate world comparing leadership and management, and usually they hold up leadership like the holy grail and denigrate management. That's because these days the corporate world is knee-deep in managers and doesn't have many good leaders. However, it's likely that you're not drowning in managers in your living room, so I'm not going to denigrate either. They are different, and you'll probably be naturally better at one than the other … and you must learn to embody both, at least to some degree.

Let's take a look at some comparisons between leadership and management, and discuss how they apply to a Master/slave relationship.

### 1. The leader's eye is on the horizon, and the manager's eye is on the bottom line.

As a Master, it's going to be your job to set the goals for the relationship, and that means being able to create the big picture. If you're bad at that, you need to get good at it. "Bad at it" can look like many different obstacles—maybe you don't know what the possibilities are because you're used to ignoring the future and pretending it isn't coming, or maybe you have lots of unrealistic ideas. For the first problem, get some therapy and learn to be an adult. For the second one, it helps to talk to people who've actually done this successfully for a long time, and ask them what they've achieved with their Master/slave relationships. The more widely varying examples you can find, the easier it will become to pick out which ones you want. Make sure that you also ask about what went wrong when they tried to implement each goal, and you can guarantee that if they're being honest, you'll hear some horror stories. That's OK—you want to know the pitfalls in the road before you step in them. It also helps to ask what didn't work out, for each couple.

On the other hand, it doesn't help to build castles in the sky that you aren't going to achieve. If you're bad at the management side of this pair, you may tend to pick goals without taking your slave's basic nature, gifts and flaws, abilities and obstacles into consideration. You may push them (and yourself) too hard and fail to notice that they're struggling—or if you do notice, you may become irritated and communicate (perhaps silently) that they have no reason to struggle, and ought to get over it. You may make plans that don't take your resources into account. Resources may include money, time, energy (yours and your slave's), outside people's willingness to help, weather, climate, politics, etc. With your eyes on the goal, you don't notice the pit that could have been avoided, and you fall in, dragging your slave with you.

For this pair, the leadership role has to come first. Even if you don't know the details of what you want your slave to do, you can still start with a clear picture and make sure that they understand it as well. It may be that you don't want to be the person who figures out the details--perhaps part of your goal for this relationship is that at least some of your arbitrary whims are catered to. However, it may not occur to you that shifting your goal a little can make things much easier, getting 90% of what you want at a much lower cost, if you're willing to compromise.

It's worth it to work out a step-by-step plan and then run it by more detail-oriented people, if this is a weak point for you. If your slave is detail-oriented, use their perspective as a resource. If they aren't strong there either, bring in an outside perspective to look the situation over and give you some tips. Other masters can help here. Remember that followers give service because it gives them faith in the future. They need both an apparently achievable goal and ongoing visible sustainability in the process. If either goes down, they lose faith and fall to the wayside.

### 2. The manager develops control, and the leader inspires trust.

In this situation, the leadership has to come first. You can't control someone who doesn't trust you, at least not in any ethical way.

You have to manifest the leadership side of this pair by showing the potential slave that you're someone who has their act together, who is solid and reliable, who keeps their promises, who is reasonably self-aware, who isn't too arrogant to see when they've made a mistake, and is willing to clean up the mess when it happens. You inspire trust by being trustworthy. This includes being honest and straightforward about areas where you've got a lot of room to improve, even if that's hard to admit. Your honesty will build trust—and if it doesn't, you've got the wrong person.

Once some basic trust is built, the management side comes in to experiment with establishing effective control. The manager thinks, "I'm going to see how you react when I use this tone of voice. OK, that went well; I'm going to give you this order and see how that works." It's important to remember that giving orders in a manner that assumes obedience can be very satisfying to a slave.

You can only get as much control as you've earned trust, though, so after that push you'll have to go back and earn more trust. These two functions work like a right foot and a left foot—take a step on this side, then take another on that side. If your right foot gets too far ahead of your left one, you'll fall down, which is what happens when attempts at control outrun the trust you've built. On the other hand, most slaves want to experience the feeling of being controlled at least some of the time, and many of them are in it almost entirely for that experience. Even if they trust you and follow you, if you never exert your active dominance, they'll miss that thrill. Some will follow along for some time because they admire and believe in you, but others may drift away, craving that hands-on experience of being actively pushed by your dominant will.

### 3. The leader motivates their people, and the manager creates rules.

Skilled leadership includes the ability to motivate someone to go along with your plans, because the end result looks rewarding to them. If you can't figure out a way to make your goals look attractive to your slave, they're going to have to figure out another way to find emotional rewards. Most slaves want to please their masters, and seeing that pleasure is a very visceral reward for them. If you're an extremely reserved person who thinks it's uncool to show your feelings, a slave may knock themselves out for what feels like little reward. Unbend and smile at them. Show your real pleasure in that great meal they cooked. Catch them doing something right, and tell them you're proud of them. You'll be surprised how far those little positive reinforcements will go in making them happy with the position.

Being an inspiring person also means working on making yourself the best *you* that you can be, and dedicating yourself to self-improvement. Sometimes the leaders that motivate people to follow and act for them are people who excel at one set of qualities or activities, and their followers are willing to overlook their other issues. However, working on your weaknesses as well as your strengths sets a good example for a slave. Remember that you may eventually want that slave to attack their limitations in order to be better at their job and role.

On the other side, slaves are in a vulnerable position, and they want to have clear boundaries and expectations regarding what is expected of them, and what they can expect of you. That's where the rules and protocols come in. They reduce vagueness, and it's important for a master to understand how distressing vagueness can be to a slave. They want solid ground under their feet. If you're not so great at this part, start with what you *can* guarantee and build on that. Maybe you can start with a list of things you know you don't want, or would never do, or never want them to do. Then flip around the "don'ts" and see if you can turn them into a "do". For example: "I hate being woken up in a loud, abrupt way; never do that to me!" can become "I want you to wake me up gently, perhaps crawling under the covers and snuggling up to me." Don't try to make too many rules at once, and remember that it's OK to discard the ones that don't work. Building up a repertoire of lasting, satisfying rules can take a long time.

### 4. The manager executes, and the leader improves.

For this pair, the management comes first. Before you can push to make improvements, you have to get things running functionally with what you've already got. This is especially important if improvements may be a high-risk or uncertain prospect. For example: The master wants the slave to learn yoga, because that's one of the master's favorite activities and it would be fun if they could do it together. The slave is disabled with physical mobility problems, and fears that it would not be possible. The master begins by having the slave practice simple range-of-motion stretches and perhaps one or two extremely simple yoga poses until those are comfortable, and then evaluates whether it is possible to go further.

The administrative part of management is about going over a process again and again until it's right. It requires consistent checking on subordinates in order to figure out how they're doing, and in fact whether they've been doing their task at all. This kind of consistency can be difficult for masters who are all about the future goals but lack the patience to regularly assess their slave's performance, which makes the slave feel as if the master doesn't really care how they perform. It's also disheartening to a slave if the master sets plans and then doesn't keep track of the tasks and projects they've assigned, which is another failure of management in this area. If this keeps happening, it can help to set outside reminders and regular check-ins. You can "tie" checking on a given task to another regular activity, using it to cue yourself. It's even possible to give the slave the job of reminding you to remind them.

When it comes to assessing how much time and effort the slave is putting into tasks when you're not around, you may want to set a "time budget". The slave is your resource; you may not need to "budget" them all the time, but sometimes it helps to allocate "time blocks" and "energy blocks". If you want tasks done (or tasks done to a higher standard) and the slave says that there's no time for it, check the time budget.

Once the basic system is in place, then you can turn to the leadership role of innovating and improving the system itself. The management side of this job finds the flaws and calibrates where the difficulties lie; the leadership side brainstorms ways to develop them. Then they get turned back over to the management side to experiment and report back. In a large corporate setting, these jobs might be split up; when it's just you and your slave in your living room, you get to do both parts—ideally with your slave's assistance. Leadership is moving forward, and you can't move forward without looking for ways to improve. Leadership also involves speculating about outside circumstances that might upend the system, and brainstorming ideas for preventative measures—having a Plan B, Plan C, and Plan D.

If you have trouble with this part of the process, it helps to get outside perspectives from multiple people who've faced this particular problem before, or do research (or assign the slave to do research) on what people have written about the obstacle. Don't' be afraid to bring in outside information; a good leader knows that they don't have all the information in the world, and they also know that they don't need to—it's out there for the finding and it's just a matter of organizing the quest.

**5. The manager cares about structure, and the leader cares about people.**

Here, like #2, both sides of the job have to work together, one right step and one left step. The management side of this dual job looks at the overall structure and asks, "Are we keeping our commitments? Are we remembering to do the important things, or do we need reminders? Are we making order-of-operations mistakes?" If there is a problem, the manager asks, "What structure could we put in place to alleviate this issue in the future?" The management job here is being invested in the *how* and the *when*.

The leader's job, on the other hand, is looking at everyone's feelings. When you're being the leader, you have to ask hard questions like: "Is this an unfair burden on my slave which may set them up for failure, or stress them to the point of unhappiness? Does my slave need some coaching or mentoring or just general support to make this work? Do they feel like they can come to me with problems, or are they trying to doggedly muddle through without letting me know about their suffering?" Alternately, you also have to ask: "Am I agreeing to this in order to make my slave happy, when it really doesn't make me happy at all? Will I be able to sustain this generosity a year from now, or will it begin to undermine my feeling of being in charge? Can I be honest with my slave about this, or will that be counterproductive? Is there anyone else I can talk to about this, and where might such a person be found?" The leadership job of this pair is being invested in the *what* and the *why*. If one side gets ahead of the other, you'll fall down. Structure has to be checked against feelings—before, during, and after implementation. Even the best structure needs to be changed if it's making someone miserable.

### 6. The manager is task-oriented; the leader delegates.

You don't have to be a paragon of organization to be a master (although it certainly helps), but you have to be able to make a list of items that are your part of the job, activities which can't be done by anyone else but the Person In Charge, and then work your way down that list and complete it. The person who never seems to finish what they've started, who easily loses interest and lets most things fall off their plate … this is someone who will drive a slave crazy, unless the slave has a strong need to "nanny" a demanding child without any authority to make them do the right thing. The managerial side of this pair is about meticulously checking off commitments, because the slave can't do their job properly if you're not doing yours. This part has to come first, because it's hard for a slave to trust and respect someone who can't come through on any of the castles in the sky that they build in glowing terms. If this is hard for you, start small—pick a number of commitments that is low enough to set you up for success, and add more slowly as you learn to be comfortable with what you've mastered so far. You might also think about getting some outside help, because if you can't keep your commitments and work through tasks that are your responsibilities, you aren't going to be a solvent adult.

Once you've proven yourself to be that responsible adult, you can begin to delegate tasks, or parts of tasks, to your slave. This may be problematic if your slave imagines their job to be one of letting go of responsibilities rather than taking them on, but unless you negotiated a "full-time parent and very young child" relationship up front, you're in it with another adult, and adults need to carry their weight. Most slaves will be proud of being their master's resource, and their self-esteem will be enhanced by their competence at assisting the master in being more effective themselves.

Just as a leader doesn't need to know it all—but only where to look, or to send someone to look—a leader doesn't need to do it all, either. However, here's where trust comes in again—in the opposite direction. The master has to trust that the slave will do their part, or they'll become wary of delegating and do it all themselves rather than risk the slave making a mess of it. A master can't comfortably let go of the reins until the slave has earned their trust. However, it's also the leader's responsibility to get the slave trained—by themselves or an outside source—to be able to do the job competently, especially if it's outside their usual talents. That may seem like more effort than it's worth, and may tempt the master to simply keep the task on their own plate, but if the slave is never challenged to do anything new, they miss the chance to stretch themselves and gain confidence in their ability to adapt to a new situation.

### 7. The manager does things right; the leader does the right thing.

This pair is the conflict between ethics and correctness, the moral code that joins both leadership and management. Once you've got rules and boundaries and protocols and commitments—all the lists of what master and slave have agreed that they will or won't do—it's the manager's job to see that it all gets done properly. As well as managing one's slave, a master needs to be their own self-manager and ride herd on their own impulses. In a very real sense, masters are doing serious behavioral management on at least two people at all times—their slaves and themselves. "Mastery" means, at its bottom, becoming really good at something. When applied to relationships, it means learning to be skilled at following the rules that have been set by and for you. Doing things right means that if you say, "We don't lie to each other," then you'll have to refrain from lying about difficult subjects to your slave, even if that's sometimes excruciating. If you say, "We will keep our promises to each other," then you need to come through even when every fiber of your being wants to be doing something else.

On the other hand, the leader needs to be constantly evaluating that same list of rules to make sure that everyone is really doing the right thing. The manager wants those rules set in stone; the leader knows that as soon as the rules start damaging someone, they must be overhauled. A good leader checks in regularly to make sure that the juggernaut that has been built is not running anyone over. If the way you've been doing things is starting to become a problem—or even if it's just no longer useful—it needs to go on the table for reflection and revision.

For example: A master has two slaves, and a definite code of rules by which Slave #1 has lived happily for many years. Slave #2 comes into the picture, and approves of the master and the rules, agreeing to live by all of them. One of those rules is that the master has the right to "lend" the slaves out sexually to other trusted and safe masters, which Slave #1 has never had a problem with. After a couple of years, however, Slave #2 comes to the master in tears and says that upon many months of reflection, they absolutely believe that this rule is against the spirit of their religious practices, and is causing them a great deal of distress. The master realizes that the right thing to do is to rescind that rule for Slave #2, even if it has long been a recognized rule in the household. Making the hard decision about the moral code of the house—and when it needs to bend or break for reasons of compassion—is part of the leadership job. While it's the manager's job to be firm and solid, it's the leader's job to be flexible. The manager part of your job can't be so rigid that the leader can't adapt when it's not the right thing to do, and the leader part of your job can't be so flexible and people-oriented that you lose the solid foundation of the relationship.

No one is good at everything, and most people lean to one side or the other, or are less than stellar at both. These skills can all be learned, though, on both sides. No matter who you are, you can become more skilled at leadership and management, even if you have to outsource some of it—again, there's no shame in delegating. You'll figure out the dance back and forth between the right side and left side, even as you once learned to walk.

*Keziah Conway is the rural-living Owner of a beautiful and intelligent piece of male human property, loves gardening, graphic novels, and fiber arts, and tries every day to be the best master possible.*

# Claiming Your Property:
# Using Marks for Ownership Dynamics
*Sinclair Sexsmith*

In many depictions of ownership dynamics, the owned person is, eventually, marked. Sometimes they have to earn it after going through a series of ordeals, sometimes they are marked when they enter into service, sometimes they are gifted it on a special occasion.

I remember holding my breath as I read the scene in *The Story of O* where O receives a brand, and, in another part, when she receives a labia piercing which holds a tag. I was fascinated: she was going to be marked *forever*. She would always have that brand, and that little scar where the piercing was, even if she took it out. It was a way to make permanent on her body the things that transformed when she was trained at Roissy, and to make permanent the time that she was owned by Sir Stephen, even if her relationship with him didn't last forever.

I've known since very early in my kink explorations that marking up someone else as a sign of ownership and dominance was really sexy to me. There is something primal about it, something that feels like it comes not from my rational, thinking brain but from some other place in my body, laying a claim on someone else. The marks are also there to give reminders of my and my boy's identities and roles to each other, and they can serve as mantras and touchstones to come back to and meditate on as we continue to bring ourselves consciously into our place with each other.

There's something taboo and dangerous about marks, too, which can be appealing. As much as we have (some) cultural acceptance of getting a lover's name tattooed, or wearing a physical object that symbolizes our commitment to each other (like a wedding ring), the taboo aspect of making a mark on someone else still can be part of the appeal. It can feel like a risk because it has the potential to expose you both, and your relationship dynamic — and for exhibitionists, or those who like to get caught, that can be a powerful part in it. Leaving marks can be like daring a submissive to take something that might be painful or scary, and leading them through it can be an exercise in trust.

But for all the reasons why we might want to play with marks, perhaps most important is that marks make the dynamic tangible. It creates a physical object, a physical experience which can be seen, smelled, tasted, touched, felt. Something psychological, your ownership dynamic, is made corporeal—and that can feel pretty magical.

Personally, my boy and I both entered into our ownership dynamic in 2011 already knowing we both had a fetish for marks. He loved (and still does) any kinds of marks I would leave on him — from canes, hands, cuttings, markers. In the nine years we've been together so far, I've left dozens of marks on him, some more permanent than others, and it has been a major way we have illustrated our dynamic.

Most Owners have some sort of experience with BDSM tools, many of which leave marks, because we're also often in the overlap of the Venn diagram with tops, sadists, and other kinds of experience creators. But if you put some intention of your ownership dynamic behind the marks you make, you can find a whole new tool in your toolbox.

When I say "marks", I mean the broadest sense of the word and concept: anything on another's body you can see, hear, smell, taste, or touch—anything you can perceive with your senses. Being able to have tangible, sensory evidence of the mark is one of the main reasons why it can have the effect of making the ownership dynamic feel more embodied.

It might be easiest to think about examples of the marks we can see, like bruises, tattoos, or specific guidelines for how to wear (or not wear) makeup. Those are the most common kinds of marks, and most marks are visible in some way, though there are occasionally marks one can feel but not see, like a bruise that hasn't surfaced on the skin. Marks we can smell or taste could be that an Owner picks the special scented soap or even all of the owned's bath products, or something like piss. Marks we can hear could be a specific kind of shoe or boot, or some specific jewelry that makes a noise when the person moves.

Thinking about marks with this broad of a definition expands what marks are, and includes all kinds of new ways to play with marks, from temporary to permanent, and from easy to difficult.

Visualize, if you will, those two scales as part of a graph: on the X axis is permanence, measuring if they last for hours, days, weeks, months, years, or decades. On the Y axis is difficulty, from relatively easy to very difficult. Marks can be placed on this chart based on how difficult they are to get and how long they last. For example, things like writing on a body with marker tend to be not very difficult and relatively impermanent. A piercing tends to last longer, because we choose to leave it in, but it is usually a relatively easy process to remove it and no longer have it, though it may leave a scar.

Though I can make some broad generalizations about what is more or less difficult, and what is more or less permanent, this chart will actually have to be very individualized. Everyone's difficulty level with different things will vary, and different activities last or affect people differently. For example, someone who plays rugby (as my boy does) can be much harder to leave bruises on, because their body is more used to being knocked around. And bruises, or even tattoos, will be different depending on the melanin in someone's skin. Someone might have a trigger around body writing, and even though writing on skin with markers is usually not painful, it could be a very intense experience for them psychologically.

My boy, for example, has a relatively high pain tolerance, and loves tattoos, so those fall on to the more easeful side of the chart. On the other hand, haircuts can be very anxiety-producing and he has definitely cried during them a few times, which can be challenging since he follows protocols of keeping his hair a certain way. I didn't know the complicated feelings that came up around gender presentation and expression when I made one of our first protocols, which was that he had to keep his hair long enough on top to grab. Yes, for blow jobs. Yes, even now, nine years later, despite the complicated feelings, he still keeps his hair how I want it.

Using this chart to lay out your s-type's personal experiences with marks will give you a lot of information about the kind of marks you can play around with and the kind of marks you approach with more consciousness.

Expanding marks to think about how they can engage our senses, and considering the ways they can be permanent, temporary, or difficult, can expand the ways we use marks. Adding intention to our marks can make them even more meaningful, and can help support and reinforce your ownership dynamic even more.

The intention we're adding can be just about anything: for example, it can be an intention to commemorate this particular anniversary or special day, or it can be a reward, it can be a milestone in the dynamic. I like to think about the relationship values in my ownership dynamic and give the marks I leave a little extra meaning.

While relationship values vary in every relationship, I have been involved in the kink and leather communities for more than 20 years, and there are some relationship values that get discussed frequently and more commonly. For us, the values of commitment, identity, and trust come up as I am playing with marks frequently, and I find them frequently discussed for others in ownership dynamics.

The obvious mark for commitment in an ownership dynamic is the collar that my boy wears. Though it is very easy to remove (if you have the key, anyway), it holds a symbol of permanence with it. I am the only one with the key, and I decide when or if it comes off, which does need to happen occasionally for things like rugby games. The collar has an auditory element—I can hear it sometimes, particularly when he is taking off his shirt or running. Before this collar, he had dog tags, and those made more noise.

We value in staying in the headspace of our dynamic, remembering who we are to each other and who we want to be, and utilizing tools to keep us there. Marks can be an excellent way to keep myself and my boy mindful about our place and intentions with our identity and roles to each other. Over the years, he has amassed multiple tattoos, piercings, and scars that have become tactile reminders of his place, like the first letter of my name tattooed on his chest, and a nipple piercing. He can touch these and remember who he is and what are arrangement is, and they are things I can see that visually remind me of both his role and my own.

Trust is a deep relationship value of ours—though not only is it an important value, it is foundational to our ownership dynamic. We are constantly bidding for each other's trust, testing trust, and building and rebuilding trust. Sometimes I think the BDSM activities we engage in are, at their core, physical games of trust that help us practice the art of trusting. Handing trust over to me also means handing me obedience and surrender, and many marks have been exercises in this arena. The boy is a particular control freak about his tattoos, as he is also a designer and an artist, and every one of his tattoos he has drawn and re-drawn until it is perfect, then Photoshopped a mock-up of it on pictures of himself, as a way to try out the options. The tattoo he has on his forearm is the Little Dipper, but it started out as intentional cigarette burns from me each time we saw each other, eventually building out the entire constellation. When I had it outlined and expanded into a tattoo, the boy didn't know what was coming or what design I had picked, and didn't even watch as the artist drew it on his body. It was a delicious exercise in trust and letting me be in complete control of a permanent mark.

As the Owner in this dynamic, I have some marks reflecting this relationship, too. (Why should the s-types get all the fun things?) When we had a collaring ceremony, I had a ring engraved with a replica of the actual key that opened the lock that went to his collar, and I wore it daily for years, until we got married and it was replaced by a wedding ring (though I do still wear it sometimes). That symbolizes my identity in this ownership dynamic as the person who holds the key. When the boy got the Little Dipper tattooed, I had the Big Dipper tattooed on myself, as a reminder of my correlating responsibilities as an Owner. When I received a formal cover, I used some of the same chain that the boy's collar was made from on the cover itself, signifying our commitment to each other.

Marks may seem like a simple thing to play with, and superficially, they can be—but they can also be expanded upon for even more meaning and value. They can be sexy, use all our senses, and make psychological dynamics tangible. Marks can be easy or difficult, temporary or permanent, and making marks can reinforce relationship values.

*Sinclair Sexsmith (they/them) is a queer butch writer focusing on queer sexualities, genders, kink, and relationships. Their short story collection, Sweet & Rough: Queer Kink Erotica, was a 2016 finalist for the Lambda Literary Award, and they are the current editor of the Best Lesbian Erotica series. Find more of their work at sugarbutch.net.*

# To Would-Be Masters Who Are Looking For A Non-Intimate Relationship

*Raven Kaldera*

But before we begin, some disclaimers!

First, I want to say up front that I am involved with multiple polyamorous relationships, with different levels of power exchange from completely egalitarian to full ownership. I *am* actually emotionally intimate with my slaveboy, but I've been in both intimate and non-intimate service relationships in my time.

Second, I should add that when I say "intimate", I mean emotionally intimate. I'm not talking about sex. Many people are capable of giving or receiving sexual service without emotional intimacy, and if you're not, you're never going to want to be in the kind of relationship I'm describing anyway, so don't worry about it. Some non-intimate relationships include sexual service, some don't. It varies.

Third: I'm not talking about SM and kinky sex. If you want a sex partner with no intimacy, you're advertising for something different—and actually, you have a lot more of a chance to get it. I'm talking about relationships where there is actually some level of real authority transfer with regard to real-world activities—the s-type's body, hair, schedule, clothing, outside sex life, job, and other activities. Each of these relationships are custom-built, but we're talking about them doing your laundry and keeping your books and escorting you to parties and monster-truck rallies, not just blowjobs.

Fourth: Many people, upon reading the title of this article, are going to cringe and want to rant about how all healthy Master/slave relationships are emotionally intimate, or should be, and those that aren't are neither healthy nor sustainable. All I can tell you, if you're having this reaction, is that you're having it from a place of your own needs and wants. For you, that's true—and that's fine. For others, a non-intimate service relationship can be a great thing. Don't judge. Instead, do a thought exercise: what sort of person would be perfectly healthy and happy in such a relationship? See if you can imagine that. It'll stretch your brain.

Anyhow, the reason I'm writing this is because I do see a lot of the wreckage from would-be or inexperienced masters who want a non-intimate relationship and go about it all wrong (including not telling the s-type that this is their intent, if they are even aware of it themselves). I know that some people want this, and will continue to keep looking for it. So this is a (by no means exhaustive) list of useful tips to help you, that would-be master, to get what you want with someone who wants the same thing, and not leave wreckage in your wake.

*1) **Be Up Front About It.*** If you are not interested in an emotionally intimate relationship where you can (eventually) show your innermost feelings and vulnerabilities, put that on the table very early in the negotiation proceedings. If you're worried that being honest about this will chase people away … well, you're shopping in the wrong pool. Believe me, it is better to let s-types who are looking for (or eventually expect to get) an intimate relationship self-select out than to go dishonestly through all the initial investment of time and effort, only to have it go sideways when they realize you're never giving them that.

*2) **Understand that what you want is a specialty item, and be prepared for a longer and wider searching period.*** Especially if you are heterosexual and looking for a female s-type (we'll get to gender differences in a moment), you will be fishing in a field full of people who want romance (and maybe marriage) along with their enslavement. For them, power exchange enhances intimacy. There are individuals who are open to what you're looking for, but they may be few and far between.

*3) **Figure out exactly what you want and don't want.*** Do some soul-searching and personal journaling on the subject. Will this be live-in or visiting? Full-time or part-time? How many areas of their life do you want authority over? What are your reasons for not wanting intimacy? PTSD? Fear? No time and energy for it in your life right now? Dislike of all that "feelings" stuff? Be honest with yourself, even if it's not flattering. Understand that the more time, energy, and investment you expect from a potential s-type, the less likely they are to settle for a non-intimate relationship. You might want to start with something only part-time, with limited control over anything that happens in their outside lives.

Also, you will need to define what you personally mean by "intimate" and "non-intimate", and where those lines are drawn. For example:

❖ Are you looking for a somewhat distant "professional" relationship?

❖ Are you looking for someone who'll be a friendly companion, but respect your space?

❖ Are you looking for someone you can have some semblance of emotional closeness or romantic relationship, but put a hard limit at a certain point of emotional involvement?

❖ Are you looking for a relationship where you can set the emotional tone as the mood strikes you, having the slave act like a romantic companion, a no-strings-attached sex partner, a devoted servant desiring to please you, or unemotionally-involved hired labor, as you choose?

❖ If you don't feel you are capable of intimacy, are you looking for this to be "training wheels" where you can have a safe space to periodically explore small, controlled doses of intimacy, without any obligation to be intimate when you aren't in a space for that? Or do you have no interest whatsoever in even considering things becoming more intimate over time?

❖ Do you specifically not want to have to deal with any of their emotions and vulnerability?

❖ Do you want access to their innermost feelings and vulnerabilities, but not give them access to yours? (*The one-sidedness isn't necessarily a bad thing, but it needs to be discussed and negotiated like everything else. Some s-types will be fine with that, some won't. Some may not know how they will react; in those cases, take it slowly and do not push for transparency.*)

If an s-type desires some level of emotional intimacy, it doesn't necessarily mean that they have a strong intrinsic desire to know their partner's deeply vulnerable issues. There are other aspects to emotional intimacy that can create that feeling of closeness. Often it is a more a desire to *be* emotionally vulnerable, and to know that their partner is emotionally engaged with them in some meaningful way. They also might want to know they are providing a supportive environment for their partner, and be concerned that their partner's unwillingness to share means they are failing at that.

However, even if a master doesn't want "emotional intimacy", there still might be a few things on this list that they either want or would not mind providing.

**4) If you are looking for a M/s relationship because you have poor relationship skills and you believe you can substitute dominance for skill, you are dead wrong.** Power dynamic relationships—like polyamory or any other "alternative" relationship—require *extra* relationship skills. It's not just a matter of you ordering and the slave doing and no other conversation is needed. This is deep stuff, even when non-emotionally-intimate, and you have to know how to get it right. Start reading up on M/s books and looking at writings by thoughtful and analytical M-types. If you want a vague technological metaphor, it's like wanting to buy and fly an airplane, if there were no airplane schools around and you had to shop for used planes on Craigslist, without actually knowing what to look for in a used plane, and never knowing what kinds of problems they might have. Guess what would happen to most of those untrained, flying-by-the-seat-of-their-pants would-be pilots in their uninspected planes? Yup. Crash. And that's what happens to new M-types who go into this thinking that it will be *easier* than an egalitarian relationship because they won't have to try as hard to figure things out.

**5) If you're not offering intimacy, what are you offering that is worth taking that off the table?** A combination of good management skills and good psychology skills can make up for it. You can also help them to achieve their life goals, or give them guidance in difficult day-to-day matters, if your own judgment is good enough. You can have a short time each week where they can vent about their life to you. You can be considerate of their personal limitations and weaknesses, which definitely helps reduce the "You don't care!" feeling. You can teach them better problem-solving skills, or get them training in skills that enrich both your life and theirs as well. You can even give them money, as a last resort. Many such boundaries are more openly negotiable if there are specific cash-for-activities involved. Before you start thinking, "But prostitution!" remember that I'm assuming that you want more than just kinky sex here. Many people hire personal assistants for all sorts of things.

**6) Don't assume that "non-intimate" means "I never tell you anything."** You will have to talk about the relationship, because all relationships develop bumps and need to be smoothed out. This is where those learned skills come in. You may have to spend time explaining your orders, because there will be little things that it won't occur to you that they need to know in order to follow your orders properly. You may have to spend time explaining the motivations behind your orders, for reason ditto. You will have to learn the difference between them questioning you because they will actually function better with more information, and questioning you because they want to argue with the order and/or get into your head out of curiosity. If you mistake the first for the second, you are shooting yourself in the foot.

You will also need to set up useful ways in which they can state their current limitations to you in ways that don't sound like arguing. If you tell them to wash the dishes, and they've got bad hand arthritis today, how can they give you this information without sounding like they are arguing? You see how this is going to require a lot of talking. That doesn't mean that it requires them to get into your personal business; you can work out these problems without that. However, if your personal demons are getting in the way of clear and understandable orders, or making them badly misinterpret your motivations, you have to take responsibility for that.

This may mean actually explaining to them, as calmly as possible, that you have Problem X, it's likely to create trouble occasionally in these places, and this is how you expect them to handle the situation.

*Remember that showing self-knowledge and self-mastery gives you more credit and respect, while looking like you aren't aware of your own problems diminishes your credit.* If the idea of talking about Problem X is too intimate, try practicing less intimate, more "declassified" ways of talking about it, preferably when you're alone. As an educator, I often speak about really painful things in front of a roomful of strangers, and I've learned to "declassify" enough of that material (by finding a way to talk about it succinctly that does not make me uncomfortable or involve emotions) to do that without ripping myself apart. It's another skill that can be learned. Nobody needs to know that you're standing in the shower practicing ways to comfortably express the minimum information your slave needs to know about Problem X in order for them to function well.

If you prefer to be vague about the details, it is generally best to describe it as dryly and succinctly as possible. Either give them a reasonably coherent full explanation, or give them nothing but a bare generalized statement. Do not lead them on with tantalizing juicy details and then refuse to explain what you are talking about. Say nothing that might lead them to believe you really want to talk to them about it, if only you could find a way. (If you think you might eventually want to talk to them about it, seriously consider whether there is any value at all in encouraging them to hope and work for that.)

**7) If you are questioned in a way or about a subject that feels too intimate, do not react from a defensive place.** Defensiveness looks weak. Instead, react from a calm, grounded space. Assume that they have unknowingly tried to open a black box that you hadn't clearly labeled. Explain where the edges of the box are, and that it is none of their concern, and how you want their behavior in this area to be.

You don't have to make a huge emotional deal out of it, but you do need some way of making it clear that this is a "hard limit" issue.

You don't have to express your emotions, but if you deflect their inquiry with a vague and noncommittal reply while concealing all trace of emotion, do not be surprised when they wander into that area again and again, continually pressing you for what is wrong or thinking you are mad at them. Be the master and make it clear what you want of them.

*Example:* Slave plays around in some way that tangentially reminds you of childhood issues the slave has no idea exist. You are clearly not amused. Slave laughs and says "Didn't you ever do that when you were a kid?"

*Response A:* Master says, "Uh ... no. I ... I'm just tired, okay?"

*Result:* Slave sulks, attempts to cheer the master up, or figure out why they are upset. The slave will continue to carelessly stomp through topics that tweak the master out, because the slave has no way of knowing what is going on.

*Response B:* Master takes a deep breath, sits the slave down, and says "I need to tell you something right now, and I need your undivided attention. You have not done anything wrong, and I am not mad at you, but I need you to understand something about me. If you bring up an issue related to my childhood, and I tell you, 'Drop it,' I want you to say 'Yes, sir/ma'am,' and not attempt to discuss the issue further. It is a huge act of trust for me to ask this of you, and at this point in our relationship I feel I can trust you to respect my wishes in this. Please do not betray my trust by pressing me on this issue or discussing it with others. There is nothing more I will say on this subject. Do you understand me?"

*Result:* Slave stares with the big deer-in-headlights eyes, and manages to say, "Yes, sir/ma'am." They know now what is expected of them.

**8) Non-sexual service, at least for the time being.** Especially if you are not looking for sex, consider hiring a service-oriented submissive from your local kink community to come over regularly to do housework, yardwork, errands, etc. It is a low-emotional-involvement arrangement where whatever D/s you provide is a "job perk" rather than the main thing, but it provides a fun and safe context to explore D/s. If you know other masters, consider an arrangement to "rent" their slave for a few hours a few times a week. It'll give you some practice dealing with an experienced submissive who is getting their primary emotional needs met elsewhere. Plus you can talk to the master about any issues, to get their feedback and perspective.

**9) *Does it have to be a girl?*** OK, if you're a straight male (or a lesbian) and you are absolutely set on including sexual service, perhaps it does. But on average there seems to be far more heterosexual men looking for this kind of relationship than there are heterosexual women desiring it. I'm not saying that there are none (especially among the singles pool), but from what I've seen the numbers don't match up. Among male s-types—and especially gay ones—there seem to be more who are OK with this. I'm also not saying that most sub men don't want intimacy—I believe that they do, but there do seem to be more of these "specialty items" among males. If you're bisexual or you could get along with a nonsexual service-only relationship, you might want to think about looking for a boy instead.

**10) *Consider looking for a polyamorous s-type with an existing primary partner.*** If they have a primary already—perhaps someone whom they love but who isn't interested in M/s—they can get their emotional needs met somewhere else and that doesn't get laid on you. This works best when they live with their primary and just come visit you part-time. In general, making sure that they have a support system and existing sources of emotional intimacy is a wise choice.

**11) *Don't take someone who seems emotionally desperate.*** They may be desperate enough to be lying (perhaps to themselves) about their ability not to fall madly in love with you and then resent you for not loving them back.

**12) *How do you know they can handle this?*** Learn effective ways to ask a potential s-type about how easily they fall in love, how they can prevent that from happening, how they will let you know if this begins to happen, etc. In order for them to give you a clear answer, they need clear knowledge of where they will and will not be allowed to tread. For example, do you want your slave to be able to:

❖ Express their own emotional vulnerability, and have that vulnerability valued and respected?

❖ Have companionable emotional closeness with the master, chatting about life and feelings and thoughts, but steering clear of "heavy" issues?

❖ Be informed when the master is in a period of distress?

❖ Be given specific (non-intimate) ways they can offer emotional support, knowing not to take it personally if the master declines, and being assured that their support is valuable when accepted, even if it seems like a small thing?

❖ Know the master values them, cares about them, and enjoys their presence?

❖ Get clear feedback from the master about the master's desires and preferences, rather than feeling like they must interpret the nuances of the master's grunts and eye movements?

❖ Respectfully express concerns regarding orders, or ask for clarification, without fear of angering the master?

❖ Make mistakes—even occasionally big mistakes—without fear of being abruptly rejected?

❖ Get praise when they do especially well? Even a stoic master can manage the occasional head pat or "Well done, girl/boy."

❖ Know that the boundaries on intimacy give the master a safe place to feel comfortable having some semblance of emotional closeness, and that a "normal" partner would not be able to provide that?

❖ Have mutually comfortable physical closeness with the master, not necessarily in the context of sex or S/M?

❖ Have opportunities to speak freely about their thoughts, feelings, and concerns, even if their normal day-to-day speech is restricted?

❖ Know the master has someone to talk to about their own issues, even if that person isn't the slave?

❖ Get a clear explanation of the master's thought process, values, and motivations, at least regarding relevant issues?

❖ Share genuinely mutually enjoyable activities, not limited to sex and S/M?

❖ Know that the master will take their emotional state into account, and will not be pointlessly hurtful to them?

***13) Understand the phenomenon of "falling in love with the dynamic".*** This happens when someone has dreamed about being in a M/s relationship for so long that when it finally happens, they have very intense emotions that resemble (or perhaps are) the "falling in love" spectrum, but in actuality they are aimed at the joy of experiencing this dynamic, not necessarily the person they are involved with. They may be unaware, or unwilling to see, that this is what's really going on. Falling in love with the dynamic has been known to make new masters and slaves stay far too long with an unsuitable partner, just because they are so desperate for the M/s. It has also made them assume that they are in love with the partner when they aren't. Even with people who are good at not falling in love with other *people*, this sort of thing can nail them. Be aware that this problem may occur.

***14) A special note for would-be M-types with Asperger Syndrome.*** I'm not saying here that all M-types who want non-intimate relationships are Aspies, nor that all Aspies want non-intimate relationships—certainly not. But there does seem to be a higher percentage of would-be M-types with Aspergers looking for non-intimate relationships than, say, in a more random sample of masters. Many Aspie M-types use a slave to control their immediate environment, so that it does not overwhelm their sensory filter. "All the candles on the mantel must be lined up in this way, exactly, every time." Others use a slave as a social interface, to play host/ess and extrovert and explain them to (and perhaps protect them from) the neurotypical people, and explain the neurotypical people to them.

If you want a slave for the first purpose, consider another ASD-type person. Make sure that you have the right sort—there's some anecdotal evidence that ASD folks come in at least two types; one type is less emotional and one is more so. (For a good discussion of these two types, please see *The Unwritten Rules of Social Relationships: Decoding Social Mysteries Through the Unique Perspectives of Autism* by Temple Grandin and Sean Barron.) You want the one that is less emotional. If you're looking for a slave for the second purpose, however, you will need a NT person, and they are going to either want an adequate (for them) level of emotional intimacy, or they will need to be finding that elsewhere on a regular basis. Please evaluate what you can and can't give, realistically, for what you need.

# Further Reading

1. Gates, Aisha-Sky. *Unequal Partnership*. Selenite Press, 2017.
2. James, Andrew. *The Way of the Pleasure Slave*. Alfred Press, 2019.
3. Kaldera, Raven. *Negotiating Your Power Dynamic Relationship*. Alfred Press, 2020.
4. Kaldera, Raven, and Joshua Tenpenny. *Dear Raven and Joshua: Questions and Answers About Master/Slave Relationships*. Alfred Press 2009.
5. Kaldera, Raven. *Paradigms of Power: Styles of Master/Slave Relationships*. Alfred Press, 2014.
6. Kaldera, Raven. *Polyamory In A Power Dynamic*. Alfred Press, 2010.
7. Kaldera, Raven, and Joshua Tenpenny. *Building the Team: Cooperative Power Dynamic Relationships*. Alfred Press, 2013.
8. Kaldera, Raven. *Sacred Power, Holy Surrender: Living A Spiritual Power Dynamic*. Alfred Press, 2011.
9. Kaldera, Raven. *Hell On Wheels: Disabled Dominants* and *Kneeling In Spirit: Disabled Submissives*. Alfred Press, 2013.
10. Kaldera, Raven. *Broken Toys: Submissives With Mental Illness or Neurological Dysfunction*, and *Mastering Mind: Dominants With Mental Illness or Neurological Dysfunction*. Alfred Press, 2014.
11. Kaldera, Raven. *Unequal By Design: Counseling Power Dynamic Relationships*. Alfred Press, 2014.
12. Parker, Christine. *Where I am Led: A Service Exploration Workbook*. Alfred Press, 2009.
13. Ms. Rika. *Uniquely Dominant: Being the Dominant in a D/S Relationship*. Lulu.com, 2019.
14. Rubel, Robert J. *Master/slave Relations: Handbook of Theory and Practice*. The Nazca Plains Corporation, 2006.
15. Tenpenny, Joshua, and Raven Kaldera. *Real Service*. Alfred Press, 2011.
16. Tenpenny, Joshua. *The Service Notebook*. Alfred Press, 2012.
17. Williams, Dan and dawn. *Living M/s: A Book for Masters, Slaves, and Their Relationships*. The Nazca Plains Corporation, 2011.

www.ingramcontent.com/pod-product-compliance
Lightning Source LLC
Chambersburg PA
CBHW022357280326
41935CB00007B/219